CULTURE
SENSITIVE
DESIGN

A GUIDE TO CULTURE IN PRACTICE

Annemiek van Boeijen
Yvo Zijlstra

BISPUBLISHERS

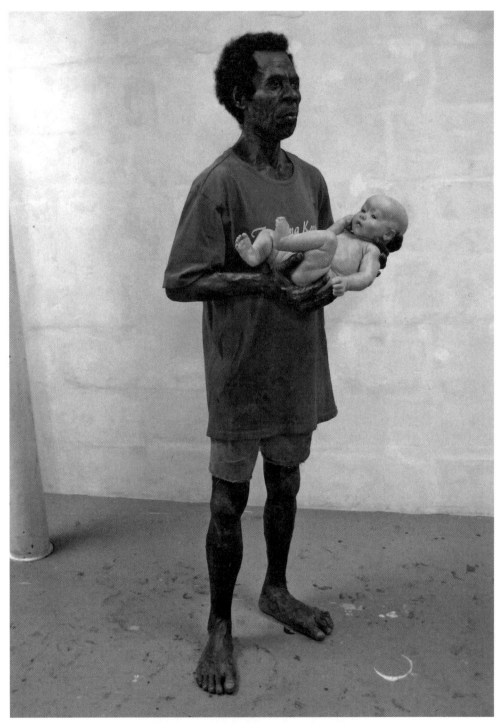

'Madonna' (after Omomá & Céline), Roy Villevoye, 2008

EVERYTHING THAT SHOULD BE LEARNED

The way we act is determined by who we are and how we have been shaped by our environment. A part of us has been formed by nature, part has been taught. It is a dichotomy that occupies us more than ever in an age of globalisation, especially when seeking to understand one another, from our different nations and cultures. We obviously cannot change what has been given to – or even imposed upon – us. But what we have been taught we can unlearn or change, or we can ensure that our children learn other things. Yet whatever the precise balance might be between nature and nurture, what is more interesting is the way we appeal to that dichotomy. The French philosopher Roland Barthes wrote that there are broadly two things we use to justify our actions: nature and history. Hunting as a hobby is a nice example: its supporters claim that hunting is both a deeply human activity and one that honours a tradition begun by our distant forebears. Both arguments hint at something beyond our control: facts that outweigh personal views on the matter, with any individual objection bound to fail in the light of it being accorded an almost divine and eternal nature. It goes without saying that this will not convince anyone who opposes hunting. 'Deeply human' can just as easily be dismissed as 'primitive'. And wasn't every tradition conceived to benefit some vested interest and rarely dates back more than a hundred years anyway? New traditions are invented all the time. The 'bucket list' phenomenon has paid lip service to this tradition-forming process in recent years, and there will no doubt be readers here who have flirted with the idea of running a marathon or taking a road trip along Route 66.

To stick with Barthes' idea, though, any appeal to either the natural self or to taught, historical cultural norms and values is a means of preferably warding off changes to behaviour or opinions; as far as the philosopher was concerned, this amounted to a damning critique of the conservative bourgeoisie. Barthes recognised that culture is inherently changeable and believed that such change ought to be channelled towards a better, even a more contemporary society. Exactly how, though? The Dutch sociologist Joop Goudsblom defined culture as 'everything that should be learned'. He was terrified of the idea of having to go through life as a second-rate nihilist, and therefore focused on what we now refer to in a somewhat cowardly fashion as 'sense-giving'. Culture, he believed, invariably contains an aspect of civilisation and, all things considered, human beings have a duty to learn what leads to civilisation.

Man Ray, The Gift, 1928

It is hard to imagine a vocation more concerned with changes in our society than that of designer. And which simultaneously asks, one would hope, what a meaningful contribution might be. Designers conceive the future. They are not merely an element of cultural changes, but must also have an active understanding of them and an ability to apply their cultural knowledge. As far as designers are concerned, therefore, what should be learned never consists of universal values of the kind pursued by psychology, say, or of the normative premises of technology or ergonomics. Design is a profoundly cultural activity, which encourages a positive contribution to the inescapable changes in the world. For that reason, this book is extremely important to every designer and can make an immense contribution to everything that should be learned.

Timo de Rijk
Director Design Museum Den Bosch

Technological innovations have shaped a new global culture that conforms itself within self-defined frameworks of standards. From a compulsion to reproduce – that lies at the core of this culture – everything needs to be registered, indexed, and stored in databases, including everything that this very system destroys. Ethnologist Frances Densmore and Blackfoot leader Mountain Chief in 1916, listening to a cylinder recording of his traditional singing for the Library of Congress.

PREFACE

The reason this book came into being is the notion that many designers regard their field as a pragmatic practice that primarily uses technological knowledge and rational principles. Projects are approached in the most efficient and systematic manner, with the aim of achieving exploitable products and services. To guarantee a successful introduction, intended users are involved intensively in the design process. Fortunately, preconditions such as ethics and sustainability are being taken increasingly into account, but strangely enough it is our own culture that makes us blind to the meaning and importance of culture in that process.

Designers who have come up with innovative solutions and unforeseen new applications are widely praised. Subsequently, intangible terms such as 'brilliance' are assigned to them, while the difference is mainly the result of a broader cultural orientation and development that opens up a world of new opportunities, insights, and possibilities.

We first need to define the concept of culture as used in this book. Culture is a collective term that consists essentially of norms and guidelines applying to social behaviour, language use, and manners that comprise the organisation of a society. Mythology, philosophy, literature, and science form the intangible, cultural heritage of a society. Material culture includes technology, architecture, and art. Design practice focuses mainly on this material culture, but no design can be viewed in isolation from the entire cultural context.

The term culture was introduced in 45 BC by the ancient Roman orator Cicero, who in his book 'Tusculanae Disputationes' described the development of the human soul as 'cultura animi', using a metaphor related to cultivating crops for the development of this supreme philosophical ideal. The difference between that and the contemporary definition is that human perfection is now sought outside of philosophy 'by all means by which man manages to escape his original barbarism through artifice.' This definition positions our culture as an antitype to our nature, and with this positioning we automatically end up in the domain of the designed world of our human existence.

On the one hand, the comprehensiveness and elusiveness of the concept can lead designers to understand the reflex of wanting to reduce it to an overview of different design styles. On the other hand, the difficult concept can lead to the view that all existing cultural differences are exaggerated,

Some of the great thinkers whose knowledge and insights in various fields have transcended cultures and times: Laozi (604 - 507 BC), Chinese philosopher and one of the founders of Taoism. Herodotus (425/420 BC), Founder of historiography with a rare knowledge of the world and its cultures in his time. Archimedes (287-212 BC), one of the greatest mathematicians. Averoes (1126-1198) Islamic lawyer, physician, and philosopher, who is seen as the founder of secularist ideas and one of the spiritual fathers of Europe.

and that a universal design language should therefore be pursued that suits everyone in all circumstances. But both forms of reductionism deny the dangers to which any form of monoculture will lead. Cultural diversity is an evolutionary necessity because of the ambiguity and dynamics required to respond naturally and effectively to changing circumstances.

Densely populated urban areas are emerging in this time of globalisation and migration. These are cultural melting pots within which new cultures and subcultures are formed from a mix of cultural influences, technological developments, and a global communication network. These changes will lead to – as yet unknown – new definitions of social organisations and economies that will lead not only to new forms of rituals, utensils, and symbols but also to a need for other design disciplines and processes.

This book is a possible response to the need to understand these cultural processes in the context of design. It provides a lens through which to look at culture (Section 1); a design-related language in which to talk about culture (Section 2); models and methods by which to understand culture (Section 3); and examples that demonstrate the impact of design (Section 4) on culture. Along with the main text, the book is richly illustrated with images and examples, supplementary to the main text and aimed at stimulating reflection and self-study.

The depiction of 'The Gift' from 1921 by artist Man Ray (page 6) is a striking example. It is an amalgam of two existing practical designs that are universally recognisable: an iron and thirteen brass thumb tacks. However, a natural meaning transforms into something extremely impractical and unreliable. The image undermines the culturally coded meaning of the objects. This unsettling experience shows that even our familiar everyday items do not serve only functional and utilitarian purposes. They determine how we interpret the world around us. In the same way, with other images and examples, we hope to elicit questions: not ones that lead to unambiguous answers, however, but new questions and thoughts that ultimately will lead to a richer understanding of what culture is and what it could mean for the process of design.

Annemiek van Boeijen, Yvo Zijlstra

CONTENTS

5 **FOREWORD**
9 **PREFACE**
13 **CONTENTS**

YOUR CULTURE:
A PERSONAL REFLECTION
17 EVERYONE ON THE SAME PAGE?
17 Why culture sensitivity in design?
18 How can we frame culture?
20 What do we mean by culture sensitivity?
23 **Five intentions for culture-sensitive design**
30 **Three reasons for culture-sensitive design**
32 **'My culture'**
41 **Your design culture**
43 **How culture sensitive are you?**

CULTURE DEFINED:
A LENS FOR VIEWING
49 STARTING POINTS
57 **How can we view culture?**
57 **Values and practices**
63 **Cultural dimensions**
65 **In what ways can we identify cultures?**
69 Global and local cultures
72 National cultures: synthetic or true
75 Subcultures: dying or booming
76 High, low, pop, and mass cultures:
   mind the stigma
79 Folk cultures: the value of traditions
80 **Between cultural groups**
80 Dominant cultures versus minority
   cultures
82 Stereotypes and archetypes
83 Value conflicts
86 Culture shock and acculturation

DESIGNING WITH CULTURE:
MODELS AND METHODS
93 LET'S GET STARTED
93 **Why models and methods?**
94 **Emic and etic: your perspective**
94 **Outsider or insider: influence of your role**
94 **Storytelling: collecting 'thick data'**
95 **Attune your methods**
96 **Language and communication**

97 **Models and methods**
98 Circuit of Culture model
101 From Persona to Cultura
105 Socio-cultural dimensions for design
109 Role mapping
111 Culture mapping with the onion model
113 Timeline past - present - future
115 Artefact analysis
117 Probes for storytelling
121 Contextmapping in cross-cultural
   situations
125 Observation
127 Interviews
128 **A smart water supply system**
130 **Designing hospital beds**

DESIGNS IN CONTEXT:
MEANING AND IMPACT
135 MAKING A DIFFERENCE
135 **The medium is the message**
136 Personal computer and the Internet
138 An iconic radio
139 Television and mass media
140 T-shirt
140 Umbrella
141 Toy bricks
142 Pointer booklets
142 The Walkman
144 Anthora coffee cup
144 Sunglasses
145 Clap skate
145 Housekeeping
146 Kitchen and cooking
147 Masks
148 Paraskevidekatriaphobia
149 Automobility
150 The wasp
151 Wheelchairs and tricycles
151 Windmills and watermills
152 Colour as a cultural code
153 Money
154 Cargo Cult

156 **REFERENCES AND FURTHER READING**
160 **COLOPHON**

Image: Oshiage, Sumida, Japan (Ryoji Iwata/Unsplash)

A PERSONAL REFLECTION

YOUR
CULTURE

The first part of this book helps you to settle into the topic of
culture-sensitive design. It explains what culture is, why it
matters, what it implies, what it determines, how it affects us in
all our daily activities and behaviour. Encourage yourself to reflect
on your own cultural background, on the design cultures you do
or do not feel part of, and on your sensitivity for cultural details.
Ask yourself how cultural sensitivity can enhance your designs,
knowing that everyone and everything is engaged in culture. It is
a defining aspect of every design assignment that we are often
unaware of. Be aware that this book is a product with a Northwest
European cultural background, written and compiled in a 21th
century technical context based on a long tradition of scientific
education.

Two activities distinguish humans from other animals: we define our identities by way of cultural signifiers and use heat or fire to prepare our food. Making tools, trading, teaching, playing competitive games, and watching television, for example, are activities that both humans and animals have in common.

EVERYONE ON THE SAME PAGE?

The aim of this book is to demonstrate the complexity of culture in a way that not only increases your understanding but also provides a hands-on means of working with it. However, this is a tricky challenge. For the sake of application, we run the risk of oversimplifying this comprehensive concept, which has been studied for so long and by so many people in various disciplines. Nevertheless, although no simple and straightforward description is possible, that is no reason not to try.

Flourishing societies are by definition multicultural. People from other cultures are constantly revealing and challenging us to question or unlearn a way of living in order to learn a way that is better by our own standards.

Why culture sensitivity in design? Although the concept is often neglected or approached only as something to consider in the case of exotic and unfamiliar situations, why is culture so important for people in general and design in particular?

This entire book is an implicit reference, and a first — not a final — attempt to answer that question. But let's start with an overall statement. The culture and cultures in which we live incorporate the most significant moral imperatives and forces that guide human actions. Cultures 'accommodate' our beliefs and ways about how to live our lives, whether as individuals or in communities, however large or small. Anyone who ignores these moral influences, or claims that culture is nothing but decor — thereby reducing it to aesthetic pleasure and entertainment — denies the most basic human and moral motives that underlie every object, activity, and social development. People may not even realise that they themselves represent a culture. As Viktor Papanek writes in his famous book Design for the Real World, next to perceptual, emotional, association-al, professional, intellectual, and environmental blocks, we have *cultural* blocks that keep us from solving tasks in new and innovative ways and endanger the designer's independent thinking *(Papanek, 1971, p.158)*.

If you want your designs to be meaningful and sustainable in a larger setting and for a specific context, and not be reduced to generating short-term — often economic — benefits, you should understand the cultures in which your designs will appear.

Cultures can develop over many thousands of years. And although we can now identify numerous undesirable situations, a great deal of wisdom often remains at the root of people's cultural values and practices. Cultures develop in a certain way and place over time. We need to understand these developments in order to arrive at design solutions that are socially smarter and more sustainable. These solutions should contribute to people's well-being: namely, not only of people that are consid-ered as individuals with their specific problems and desires but also of members of groups and entire systems that include non-human entities as well.

If you want to understand aspects of the world around you, your culture-sensitive development must be broad and, in particular, include history. You need to be interested in all kinds of manifestations of culture; this means not only in creative expressions such as in literature, music, film, fine arts, architecture, fashion, and other forms of design but also in manifestations of everyday life. This development of cultural awareness and sensitivity can only proceed from a keen sense of curiousity, an open mind, and a sustained, wide interest in social and cultural matters.

The cultural anthropologist Franz Boas was one of the first researchers to state that pre-modern societies, referred to as 'primitive', have cultures in exactly the same way that modern societies have them. In the 19th century, 'culture' was generally regarded as an attainment that societies acquired as they advanced in marked levels of civilisation. This has proven to be wrong. There are many different people but there is only one humankind.

It is human nature to have culture. Other species are programmed to 'know' how to cope with the world, but our biological endowment evolved to allow us to choose how to respond to our environment. We can't rely on our instincts; we need an instruction manual. And culture is the manual.[1]

How can we frame culture? Let us start with a definition. The term is a comprehensive one and can be interpreted in many ways. In 1952, Alfred Kroeber and Clyde Kluckhohn had already listed 164 definitions of culture found in the anthropology literature. A common starting point in these is that people are perceived as being members of groups that have a common ground, a shared understanding of how to deal with each other.

In 1973 the cultural anthropologist Clifford Geertz looked at culture as a set of control mechanisms – plans, procedures, rules, and instructions – for regulating human behaviour. He emphasised the role of symbols in constructing the shared meaning. And he used the term 'thick description' to emphasise that culture needs to be understood from a comprehensive and deeper perspective regarding human behaviour in its specific context. In line with his approach, and also useful for design, in 1976 Bates and Plog defined culture as: 'The system of shared beliefs, values, customs, behaviours, and artefacts that the members of a society use to cope with their world and with one another, and that are transmitted from generation to generation through learning'.

Within a society, members can be grouped in many different ways: for example, by nation, profession, generation, hobbies, family, religion, and so forth. During our lifetime, we live in various groups in different places, and in each group, we take on different roles, such as parent, friend, colleague, and neighbour. In the context in which these roles are performed, we can therefore speak of family cultures, corporate cultures, sport cultures, and so on. And in each group, through language, symbols, rituals, and more, we learn about how to relate to each other. In these groups, products and services as well as other designed manifestations play a symbolic role. They are part of our 'material culture', and have not only utilitarian functions, making our lives more comfortable and safer, but also a social meaning; they tell us – both as individuals and as a group – where we come from, who we are, and who we want to be, and they affect the ways we deal with each other. Consequently, products and services influence these relationships.

After the introduction of the bicycle at the end of the 19th century, its users, known as 'wheelmen', were challenged by rutted roads of gravel and dirt, and faced antagonism from horse riders, wagon drivers, and walkers. Cycling as a recreation became organised shortly after racing did. In its early days, this brought men and women together in an unchaperoned manner, particularly after the invention of the Rover Safety bicycle. Public cries of alarm at the prospect of moral chaos arose from this and from the evolution of women's cycling attire, which grew progressively less restrictive and offered less coverage.

Nowadays, the social and political debates all seem to focus on identity. It appears to be a concept that lies beyond both culture and biology. Is identity innate, or is it socially constructed? Is it determined or can it be chosen? Are our identities defined by the existing state of social relations, or do we carry them with us wherever we go?

In contrast to nature, we could say that culture is not *inherited* but is *learned*. It is influenced by nature but nurtured by people. Culture is not necessarily transmitted over a very long time (from generation to generation, as in Bates and Plog's definition), but can also be seen as a dynamic process that develops over a shorter period. For example, if you form a team to carry out a design project, you will agree on what is and what is not important, and you will share a certain way of working. Together, you develop a team culture, a business culture, or a subculture.

A useful visualisation as to how designers could view culture is the pyramid with three levels, each of which functions as a kind of lens. In addition to the group level, two other levels are distinguished that can help make clear how to look at people in different ways; these are the individual level, where human characteristics can be either inherited or learned, and the universal level, where characteristics are based on human nature, and are inherited only. How can we link these distinctions to the practice of design? These distinctions are shown in the development of bicycle design and its use and acceptance in society.

▸ *The individual level:* The bicycle can be viewed as a product designed to match the preference of single users. The designer does not necessarily address a specific cultural group in mind but focuses on what individual people prefer. In this theoretical model, the individual and cultural levels are separated, but in practice this is problematic. Regardless of whether they like it or not, individual people are influenced by cultures, and the designer cannot design in a way that ignores culture, because he or she also belongs to a culture. Therefore, culture cannot be separated from the individual *(de Mooij, 2004; Hellemans, 2014, p.88).*

▸ *The group level:* The bicycle can be seen as a product that represents specific values or an identity for a particular culture or cultural group. For example, the widespread use or a typical local configuration of a bicycle can become a national symbol like the 'Dutch bike'. Although the bicycle in general has a strong Dutch association, the

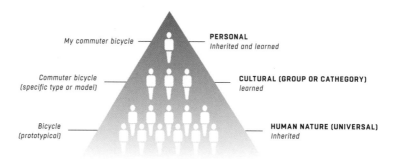

My commuter bicycle —— **PERSONAL**
Inherited and learned

Commuter bicycle ——— **CULTURAL (GROUP OR CATHEGORY)**
(specific type or model) *learned*

Bicycle ——— **HUMAN NATURE (UNIVERSAL)**
(prototypical) *Inherited*

Three lenses through which to view people on three different levels and what it means for design. The designer's attention is drawn to different aspects of the design, depending on the lens. The border between personal and cultural is depicted as a squiggly line to indicate that they are difficult to separate. (after Hofstede, 1997)

design in fact originates from the United Kingdom *(Sardar, 2012, p. 19)*. Such a meaning is learned and not inherited; the bicycle can only be typified as Dutch if people inform you of this by way of language.

▸ *The universal level:* The bicycle can be seen as an efficient way of using human energy for transport purposes. Universal design characteristics are being applied when they are based mainly on characteristics relating to *human nature*: physical capacities, utilitarian needs, and the available technology that can support these needs. In the example of the bicycle, the configuration is based on people's physical capabilities, which are independent of a cultural group.

▸ *The pyramid metaphor:* is meaningful for designers when they examine a culture, but can be understood in terms of a certain existing hierarchy of importance. Each level is important for designers, and the intended users of their designs should be studied closely on each level. That is why the designer is placed in the centre of the three lenses. Depending on the project, one lens might be more important than another one.

'We can't see our way of life from the inside, just as we can't see our own faces. The culture of the 'other' serves as a looking glass.'
(Frans Boaz)

What do we mean by culture sensitivity? Culture sensitivity is the competence to be aware of and to experience differences and similarities between people – their values and practices – and that are based on what they have learned as members of groups. The starting point for culture sensitivity is to have an open and flexible mind, and to be able to change perspective from your own to that of other people's, because this improves your empathy and leads to better solutions that support the well-being of both the individual and the group.

Culture sensitivity – or intercultural sensitivity if you want to emphasise the interaction between two or more cultural groups – is the genuine interest in the cultures of others together with an interest in interpreting signals from others. The goal of the culture-sensitive designer is to know what the values, needs, and desires of the intended users really are, based on who they are as part of a cultural group. In 2004, Milton Bennett developed a model that shows six different stages relating to people's intercultural competence, and is designed to help you reflect on your proficiency in terms of being culture sensitive. The idea is that people can move from ethnocentrism to ethnorelativism in six stages of experience: Denial; Defence; Minimisation; Acceptance; Adaptation; and Integration.

In colonial times, European travellers judged different languages on the basis of whether they understood them or not. They largely defining them as being inferior and primitive. They responded in similar ways to unknown religions and symbolisms, which resulted in contempt for other cultures and their people.

Ethnocentrism refers to the experience of perceiving one's own culture as being central to reality. Beliefs and behaviour to which people become accustomed in their primary socialisation experiences are unquestioned; they are experienced as being 'just the way things are'. Ethnorelativism is the opposite of ethnocentrism, and means that one's own beliefs and behaviour are experienced as simply one organisation of reality among many viable possibilities. After reading the explanations of the different stages, you can ask yourself: Which stage best reflects my attitude and abilities with regard to cultures?

Although most people develop their sensitivity through personal experiences of culture-related encounters, it can also be trained. It starts with awareness. The fact that you are reading this book already proves your cognisance of the role of culture in design. You can also do the Intercultural Readiness Check *(IRC-Center, n.d., Brinkman and Weerdenburg, 2014)*, a tool that checks your Intercultural Sensitivity, which is defined as the degree to which a person takes an active interest in others as well as in their cultural background, needs, and points of view. The other tested aspects are Building Commitment, Intercultural Communication, and Managing Uncertainty.

The model and tool focus on the direct interaction between people, in terms of what they say and how they behave. Less attention is paid to the things – the material culture that is our created world – that influence these interactions. Obviously, for designers, the material culture plays a role in their sensitivity as regards the meaning

The Developmental Model of Intercultural Sensitivity (DMIS) (Milton Bennett, 2004) explains how a person experiences his or her own culture in relation to other cultures.

In the most reductive version of the new biologism, life is programmed, and culture is simply the interface. Even the most popular social science, such as behavioural economics, is based on human nature. The notion of nurture is out of fashion.

of things that surround people: for example, what they wear and how products and services influence their daily lives.

▶ *Denial: You experience your own culture as the only 'real' one.* Other cultures are either not noticed at all or are understood in a vague manner. People in this stage are generally uninterested in cultural differences.

▶ *Defence: Your own culture is experienced as the most 'viable' or 'evolved' one.* People at the Defence level, in contrast to Denial, do experience the existence of different cultures. However, they do not experience these cultures as being equal to their own, which results in dualistic *us* versus *them* thinking, and is accompanied by negative stereotyping.

▶ *Minimisation: Your experience of universal similarities overrides the experience of differences.* People in the Minimisation stage recognise superficial cultural differences in food, customs, and so on, but they emphasise human similarities in physical structure, psychological needs, and/or assumed adherence to universal values.

▶ *Acceptance: You experience your culture as one of a number of equally complex and human worldviews.* Your self-reflective perspective allows you to accept the existence of culturally different ways of organising human existence, although you may not necessarily like or agree with each of the ways. You can identify how culture affects a wide range of human experience, and you have a framework for organising observations of cultural differences. We recognise people in this stage through their eager questioning of others. This reflects a real desire to be informed, to learn about 'the other', and not to confirm prejudices.

▶ *Adaptation: You are able to expand your own worldview to accurately understand other cultures and to behave in a variety of culturally effective ways.* You make constructive use of empathy, and your frame of reference is shifting to enable you to understand and to be understood across cultural boundaries. It is the ability to act effectively outside of one's own culture that forms the basis of biculturality or multiculturality.

▶ *Integration: Your experience of self is expanded to include the movement in and out of different cultural worldviews.* At this level, you have a definition of self that is not central but is *marginal* to any particular culture. This allows you to shift smoothly from one cultural worldview to another, without losing your own perspective in terms of values and practices that are rooted or developed in the culture(s) that you were raised in or lived in.

Ethnocentrism is rooted in colonialism. Great Britain, which ruled the largest colonial empire in human history, based its right to dominate on its alleged cultural and moral superiority. The Treaty of Allahabad marked the beginning of British rule in India on 12 August 1765. Between 1815 and 1914, a period referred to as Britain's 'imperial century', around 10 million square miles (26 million km²) of territory and roughly 400 million people were added to the British Empire.

Five intentions for culture-sensitive design

This section provides a brief introduction to what is meant by culture sensitivity in the context of the design discipline. As a culture-sensitive designer, you may wonder what the effect of your design could be on the culture in which your product, service, or other design intervention will appear. Assuming that cultures are difficult to change through design, your influence might be minimal. Nevertheless, consciously or unconsciously, you will design with a certain *intention* in mind. After all, most designers want to change something for the better, right? In essence, designers see opportunities for improvement in a current situation, and/or they have a vision relating to a desired future. Culture-sensitive designers are conscious of the effect that their design could have on a culture, and of what is considered 'good' and 'bad'. By the same token, culture-sensitive designers are aware of how the culture they are designing in influences their opinions about what constitutes good design.

There are five possible intentions to be considered in dealing with culture. They are called intentions – and not, for example, aims or strategies – to emphasise that they simply provide a direction and are not a fixed end result. You can use these intentions as a checklist to position yourself and to discuss your position with other people involved.

The sound system concept started in the 1940s, in the parish of Kingston, Jamaica. DJs would load up a truck with a generator, turntables, and huge speakers to set up street parties. They initial;y played American rhythm and blues music, but gradually more local music was created. Custom-built systems began to appear from the workshops of specialists, capable of playing bass frequencies at 30,000 Watts or more. Immigrants brought the sound system to London and New York, together with 'toasters' who rapped over the records, thus kicking off hip-hop.

Affirm a culture - To affirm a culture means here that your intention is to affirm the existing cultural values of the group in question. The designer looks at how she or he can enhance and affirm the culture of his or her intended users: for example, the design supports and strengthens the culture's identity, and consequently gives its members a sense of belonging. Souvenirs and fanclub items typically are designed to affirm the cultural identity of countries, cities, and sport clubs, but these are superficial examples of what design can do. The affirmation of a culture can also be subtler. For instance, by applying decorative elements from a cultural heritage in a meaningful way you could communicate a shared history. Or, in a culture where gender equality is important, the culture could be affirmed by designing something that includes usage by all genders, not emphasising a specific category. In a strongly individualistic culture, the culture could be affirmed by way of products and services for highly individual usage (think of the i-phone, i-pads, and so on).

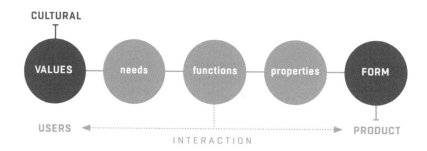

Reasoning model (after Roozenburg and Eekels, 1995)

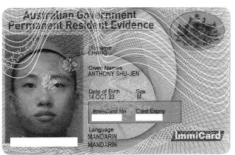

The colour green is most commonly associated with nature, life, health, youth, spring, hope, good fortune, and jealousy. Political groups advocating environmental protection describe themselves as part of the Green movement. Green is the colour of safety and permission; a green light means go ahead, a green card permits permanent residence. In Western countries, green can also be associated with toxicity.

The colour green has a number of traditional associations in Islam and the Quran, where it is associated with paradise. In the 12th century, the Shiite Fatimids chose green as a dynastic colour, but it is also widely used in Sunni states, notably in the flag of Saudi Arabia.

Attune to a culture - Attuning to a culture means that your intention focuses on the attempt to be in tune with existing cultural values in order to achieve an optimal design and to avoid mismatches between the cultural group and the product. By checking the perception of forms and functions, the designer remains alert to the possibility of misinterpretations. When it comes to culture, the designer's goal is to avoid possible mismatches between design and intended users. Some examples that typically need checking to avoid mismatches in cross-cultural design projects are listed below, structured according to the reasoning model of Norbert Roozenburg and Johannes Eekels *(van Boeijen et al., 2013, p.16)*

▸ *Forms:* Colours, materials, textures, sizes, decorations, and so forth can be interpreted in a variety of ways in different cultures. In Japan and South Korea, for instance, the power button on a remote control is red, while in Western countries it is green. The basic form – or archetype – that represents a certain product category can be different as well. A new insect repellent lamp designed for rural India was modelled on mobile lamps that were already familiar to the intended users.

▸ *Properties:* Due to its form, a product has certain properties such as weight, strength, or comfort. Properties describe the expected behaviour of a product under certain cir-

AFFIRM A CULTURE	ATTUNE A CULTURE	CHANGE A CULTURE	ABRIDGE CULTURES	BYPASS CULTURE
How can existing values be affirmed by design?	*How to avoid mismatches between a cultural group and a design?*	*How can existing cultural values be changed by design?*	*How can different cultural values be bridged by design?*	*How to define another focus to bypass cultural aspects?*

A list to position your design project; what intentions and considerations are most appropriate and important?

In China, good fortune is related to the colour red. In Chinese stock exchange graphs, for instance, red indicates trading is low, whereas green indicates the opposite. In the West, the colours mean the reverse. This could lead to some alarm if, for instance, a stock trader visiting from the East was not aware the colours meant something different in the West.

Dishwashers were initially launched in the China market in the early 1990s but failed to become popular. Consumers thought these machines were not essential, thought installing them was troublesome, or doubted their efficiency. in contrast to the West where about 70 percent of European and American families had dishwashers only 0.5 percent of Chinese families bought one.[2]

cumstances. For example, a lightweight, expensive electronic device can be perceived to be cheap and unreliable in one culture, while in another it is considered advanced and luxurious.

▸ *Functions:* The utilitarian functions of a product — what people can do with it — can be specific for a cultural group. For example, a dishwasher for the Chinese market needs handy storage areas for bowls of different sizes. The first dishwashers, attuned only to food cultures in Europe and North America, were designed with a main storage section for plates. Functions can also be social: for instance, to communicate people's social status in the group.

▸ *Interactions:* People have learned to interact with their world (e.g. for reading, writing, and behaving in traffic) in a certain way, and these interactions become conventions and routines that are difficult to change. A recipe might be easily followed in countries where people are used to reading from right to left, whereas it would be difficult to follow in countries where people are accustomed to reading from left to right. Therefore, it is important to take these conventions into account. A famous example demonstrating a design concept that went wrong was the advertisement of a brand of milk powder. The narrative began with a mother and baby. In the first picture, the baby looked sad; in the second one, the baby was drinking the milk; and in the third picture, the baby was laughing and the mother looked pleased. People interpreted the story negatively, however, because they read it in the unintended direction, following the conventions they were used to (i.e. from right to left).

▸ *Needs:* The dishwasher example for functions fulfils the need to have clean tableware. For most cultures, this need might be the same. On a more detailed level, however, the need could be different: for example, the need for a certain storage space may be influenced by the number of people who usually have dinner together (e.g. large versus small families).

Nike's 'flaming air' logo caused outrage in parts of the Muslim world because the design that was supposed to look like flames resembled the word 'Allah'. As well as issuing an apology, Nike withdrew 38,000 pairs of the basketball shoes worldwide. The The Pro-Hijab sportswear for athletes that the company launched at the 2016 Olympics was more successful.

▸ *Values:* How people finally value a product is influenced by the cultural context in which they have learned about what is morally right and wrong, good or bad, beautiful or ugly. These are cultural values. For the dishwasher example, you could, for instance, ask people what moral considerations they have about water and energy consumption (sustainability issues); about the value of doing the dishes together as a form of social cohesion; or about other shared values that influence people's needs and consequently lead to other functions, properties, and forms.

Obviously, companies are keen to avoid cultural mismatches. This is not only because their products will not be purchased but − even more important − also because their cultural biases lead to negative criticism that is spelled out in the media, and results in damage to their public image. An example is Chanel's very expensive black wood and resin boomerang, which was heavily criticised by Australian aboriginals. They were severely offended that an icon representing their deeply rooted, millennia-old cultural heritage had been appropriated and was being sold as a luxury item at an exorbitant price. Another example is Nike shoes with a graphic that was similar to the way the word Allah is written in Arabic. Therefore, to a certain extent your design needs to be attuned to the targeted culture(s) to ensure that it will be accepted or − even more crucial − to ensure that it will be *loved*.

Change a culture - To change a culture means having the intention to change a current socio-cultural value by means of a design. Products influence people's lives − if they let them − and it is a designer's challenge − maybe even *responsibility* − to determine how to achieve this. Products offer new practical functions, such as mobile communication or a fast and comfortable way to get from A to B, but they also mediate in how we deal with each other in our social interactions. Products communicate who we are, our values, what we consider to be important, and our social status. Your design may address values that are different from those that are generally accepted by the cultur-

Presentation matters. 'Les Sapeurs', or members of the 'Societe des Ambianceurs et des Personnes Elegantes', began as one of emulation. Congolese men who worked for the French colonisers, or spent time in France, began to adopt that country's sartorial elegance and aristocratic manner. The bicycle ambulance in rural areas of Malawi is designed to transport patients in a slightly raised position, since a horizontal position would indicate the person was dead.

Some designers make an enormous effort to design for areas where people cannot afford the products designed for and sold at the top of the economic pyramid.

al group. For example, let us say that gender roles in your targeted culture are strictly separated, with men and women having different rules by which they are expected to live their lives. You could then approach things with the intention of making these roles more equal by designing something that would be easy to accept and desired by both men and women. For example, a large and tough-looking baby carrier could – for some men – lower their resistance to using it.

Bridging two or more cultures - Bridging two or more cultures could be an intention if you want to elicit cooperation and respect between cultures through design. For instance, the European flag and the anthem 'Ode an die Freude' – based on the last movement of Beethoven's 9th Symphony, composed in 1823 – are two symbols introduced in an attempt to build a bridge and to unite disparate cultures that are divided into different nations. Especially in those public spaces where cultures converge, there are many occasions for designers to bridge cultures through design.

A strategy to bridge two different cultures through design could be to combine products from both cultures and translate the result into a new product category. One example is the burkini, which combines the burka with a bikini, while another is Bollywood, which combines Bombay with Hollywood.

Bypass culture in design - Bypass means that you focus consciously on other aspects of design, such as the individual or universal perspective of human behaviour. This fifth and last direction circumvents cultural values simply because, for example, stakeholders' priorities, including the designer's, are different. You have no culture-specific intention in mind. One might, in fact, wonder whether it is even possible to design free of culture-related considerations, because the culture you are in and your own cultural background are inseparably connected to you. But at least you could consciously decide not to pay too much attention to the notion of culture sensitivity,

Avoiding confrontation, saving face, and maintaining harmony are among the values that influence how the Japanese communicate anything they think could be upsetting to another person. This is in stark contrast to the confronting American approach, which makes conflict or miscommunication between east and west seem almost unavoidable. All cultures look for opportunities to evaluate each other's character. When Japanese share gifts, it is customary to refuse the gift politely several times before accepting it. Americans prefer a more competitive approach in building relations, like playing golf.

Meetings are not for brainstorming or decisions. In general, Americans send one or two people to a meeting to tell you everything they think you need to know. Conversely, The Japanese send 20 people to a meeting to learn everything you know.

or even strive for a global solution. Many design projects do not relate explicitly to culture. However, even in these projects culture plays a role whether you like it or not. A case in point is the design of the rollercoaster. It was found that whereas Western riders mostly waved their arms in the air while the ride was swooping and twisting in various directions, the Japanese tended to bend forwards, which resulted in injuries. Adjustments had to be made in order to make the rollercoaster suitable for Japanese riders *(Trompenaars and Hampden-Turner, 1998).*

Intentions for good or for bad - Every theory, technology, or product that has been developed for the purpose of bettering the world can also be used against people, and in ways that exclude and suppress specific groups. There are many instances in which design has been used to unite and persuade people to 'join the club', sharing specific values, beliefs, rules, and practices. Religious, ideological, and political groups have used products as symbolic means that expressed the values that the groups represented. In the Second World War, design was used to refer to a desired past by using classicistic architecture and inducing people to believe in a better future. Classic elements of architecture, uniforms, and other products as well as the re-use of old typography and symbols — such as the swastika — were used in new rituals to affirm certain values and beliefs that evoked a false perception of a better past. The consistent use of a specific form of language in design contributed to the development of a group identity, which was needed to give people a sense of belonging. In a business context, we could call this process *branding*, in that it is an affirmation of an identity through product design. Nowadays, product design is still used to include and exclude groups. Therefore, culture-sensitive design must not be seen as simply a hobby for designers who are curious about 'otherness'; it should, in particular, be seen as a requirement to identify the positive and negative role of design in cultural processes.

Three reasons for culture-sensitive design

The pragmatic reason that designers often give when asked why they should study cultures is to avoid mismatches between products and their targeted users. There are, however, other compelling reasons in the design process that you could consider important. A few particularly outstanding ones are listed here.

Being an autonomous individual with a coherent identity and sense of free will is an illusion. This self-illusion is probably an inescapable experience necessary for interacting with others and the world, and indeed we cannot readily abandon or ignore its influence. Nevertheless, we should be sceptical about the notion that each of us is the coherent, integrated entity we assume ourselves to be.

Cross the chasm in order to connect - Your cultural sensitivity will help you to cross the cultural chasm that might exist between you and your stakeholders. Not only do your designs need to be attuned but the design research methods, communication, and persuading strategies that you use during the design process also need to be attuned to the different situations. Culture sensitivity in this way enhances your empathy and respect for the people you are working with. Erin Meyer offers an anecdote involving a collaboration between people from different cultural backgrounds that illustrates the need to be sensitive with regard to other cultures and their influences: 'I attended a meeting the other day in Paris with a group of my France-based employees and one of our Parisian clients. As the meeting was clearly winding down, I awaited the final 'Here's what we've decided' recap of the meeting. Instead, one of the clients announced dramatically, 'Et voilà!' [There it is!], as if everything had been made clear. The others all stood up patting one another on the back and shaking hands, uttering words of appreciation and speaking of future collaborations. I couldn't help but wonder, 'But voilà what?' It seems that my French colleagues simply know what has been decided and who should do what without going through all of the levels of clarification that we are used to in the United Kingdom.' *(Meyer, 2016; p. 46)*. You can find many such examples in the literature in the field of cross-cultural management and communication. Section 3 demonstrates how insights gleaned from these disciplines are translated into guidelines for methods and tools for designing.

Gain a deep understanding of intended users - Currently, many user-research methods help designers to gain an understanding of individual persons. However, people influence each other and share common ground in order to be able to deal with each other. Culture sensitivity helps us to see what is personal, what is influenced by the cultural and societal context, and what aspects of human behaviour are universal. This bigger picture leads to a deeper understanding that helps in the development of a design vision. Using this approach, you can anticipate or steer the *effect* that the new design may have on the context and the culture that people live in. You develop this skill by being *consciously* culture sensitive, which will make it more likely that you will create culture-sensitive designs in the future.

In her studies on empathetic understanding in user research with regard to cross-cultural design, Chen Hao found that design teams sometimes fail to recognise the important triggers for this type of understanding. In user research on bathroom products, the quote from a Chinese user — 'my first salary to buy my parents a premium bathroom product to show them my love and devotion' — was not immediately recognised by the German designers as an important expression of filial piety, a core cultural value that underpins the close and affectionate ties between children and parents in China *(Hao et al., 2017)*.

Be inspired to find new ideas - When we look at the history of civilisation, we see that people have always been inspired by practices from other cultures. New products, music, architecture, and other creations arise by copying, adjusting, and combining existing design manifestations from different places around the world. Designers can

Inspired by Roman baths, the hammam developed in the Ottoman Empire, the Maghreb, and as far as the Middle East. It is a place of purification for body and mind – a meeting place that allows you to get rid of stress and toxins, and to emerge clean and calm. The steam helps deep-clean the skin and eliminates toxins and bacteria. After your session, you are taken to a cool room where tea is offered. Compared to cultures where bathing is both a meaningful and social ritual, current morning shower routines reflect a strict idea about hygiene and structuring the day.

make use of these differences to find new ideas. For instance, in a project for the development of a new and more sustainable way of bathing, designers studied different types of bathing cultures *(Kuijer, 2014)*, such as Asian bucket bathing and the European way of bathing and showering. The result was 'Splash', a combination of showering and washing with a bowl.

The Senseo coffee machine is another example that was typically inspired and influenced by two distinct cultures. The design blends Dutch coffee drinking habits with Italian practices: Dutch pragmatism – a quick and easy single serving of coffee, not too strong – with the creamy foam that comes with an Italian espresso. For some members of the respective group, it was a convenient step to improve their coffee culture, while for others it was an in-between step towards the authentic Italian coffee culture.

Different products, behaviour, beliefs, and values are a tremendous inspiration. They help to deconstruct conventions and lead to rethinking the current situation.

A deep understanding of why people do what they do can be a great inspiration for new product ideas. I take the squatting bowl-toilet as a case in point. People in diverse cultures address their toilet needs differently. They squat or sit. At first glance, squatting seems to be the common way people in economically disadvantaged areas go to the toilet, and a bowl toilet is often seen as a symbol of economic development. But

Through Western eyes, a squat toilet can seem cumbersome, intimidating, or just gross. But those are the same words used by squatters for a Western-style toilet, which they consider weird and unhygienic. According to the UN, one-third of the global population lacks 'improved sanitation'. Which means they probably rely on a bucket or a pit latrine, leading to rampant disease. In many parts of the world, the Western toilet is a symbol of wealth or a necessity for people who are overweight or have stiff joints. Japanese toilets are marvels of technological innovation and status. They have integrated bidets, dryers, and heated seats; they clean themselves, deodorise the air, and fill the stall or room with the sound of rain for relaxation and privacy.

Any parent engaged in potty training an infant knows well that everyone has to be taught how to use a toilet. people who are used to squatting often prefer this way, and even with a toilet bowl at their disposal they will stand on the toilet seat. Airline cabin-crew staff complained that sometimes while *en route* to certain destinations, passengers make the toilet seats dirty by crouching on them. However, a closer study revealed that in fact the squatting position is very healthy, because the intestines are in a better position when the person is crouched. This led designers to consider how the benefits of a bowl toilet and a squatting toilet could be combined, and voilà! – a new design was born.

'My culture'

What is 'my culture'? If people ask *'Where are you from?'*, they would probably like to know more about who you are from a cultural perspective. They ask implicitly about your cultural background in order to understand how you think and behave, to know to which 'tribe' you belong to, and what values and beliefs you share. The place where you lived during your childhood, and for what period of time, tells us something about your cultural identity. This information is useful for others if it helps them to anticipate your behaviour and to find points of entry for a conversation.

The tricky thing, however, is that you as an individual do not necessarily represent the cultural group 'you are from'. You may even have wrested yourself away from what others call your culture. Therefore, what can now be seen as *'my culture'* is actually formed over time through many personal experiences, and to describe or

To maintain their identity, sports fans follow a particular team, experiencing a positive emotion when their team wins or their rival team loses. As identification blossoms, fans begin to correlate their social identity with the performance of athletes and sports teams. Viewing sports provides individuals with something grander than themselves that they can feel a part of without requiring any special skills, knowledge, or acceptance of particular institutional values.

it remains common to see the Weird as 'normal' – or at least as a 'standard' – against which other cultures, and people, are judged.[3]

explain that is complex. A simple answer to the question 'Where are you from?' can therefore be easily misinterpreted. '*Ah, you are from..., okay... .*' And with that, you feel you have been placed in a box and stereotyped, and not really seen as the person you consider yourself to be. Especially in strongly individualised societies, people want to be viewed as individuals and not associated directly with the culture in which they were raised. Nevertheless, it is also possible that you do not feel comfortable talking about the place in which you were born. You might prefer the sense of belonging to the particular place and time in which you still live or grew up. It feels familiar and safe, especially if you are fortunate enough to look back on positive experiences. An encounter with a stranger who appears to be from the same culture might even become a feast of recognition while sharing anecdotes about the specific place and time. The designed environment plays a significant role in perpetuating this recognition.

Personal identity in relation to culture - The question 'Where are you from?' also refers to a person's identity. It is asking who you are in relation to others, and to how other people can identify you as both an individual and part of a specific group. The answer involves characteristics of the self that are unique, that apply to you specifically, as well as characteristics that are not unique but similar to others, and that therefore can be recognised and categorised. As a result, both uniqueness and sameness play a role in the construction of our identity. We learn about our own identity and the identity of others through interactions with family, peers, organisations, institutions,

33

The selfie is a persons statement to the world to stand out or to prove to be a part of something. In Chinese society people value social identification. Pursuing personal freedom, which includes extreme sports, is bound to face more challenges than in other countries. An extreme example is rooftopping. A selfie taken by a Celebes crested macaque in mid-2014 was at the centre of a debate over the copyright status of images created by animals, raising questions both about identity and intellectual property.

Example of an identity divided into ascribed and achieved identity characteristics that contribute to the story about your identity. Ascribed: Female, Indian, Gujarati Hindu, dark haired, right-handed. Achieved: designer, traveller, reader, multilingual, empathetic, exceptive to emotions, sensitive, yoga practitioner, mediator.

media, and whatever other connections we make in our everyday lives. Your identity is therefore formed on the basis of the various experiences that you have during your lifetime, and culture plays a role in this.

Philosophers, sociologists, and other behavioural scientists have studied the concept of personal identity, and diverse discourses exist. We like to perceive 'identity' as a socially and historically constructed story that helps us to distinguish one person from another, and to deal with others and ourselves. The story about who you are is fluid; it is not fixed, and it develops over time. It can be different in various situations, and depends on the diverse roles you have (such as a daughter in your family or a colleague at work). The story about your identity is not even a fixed truth, though parts of your identity are stable, and difficult to change. Marieke de Mooij (de Mooij, 2004) distinguishes identity and image, with identity being the idea one has about oneself, while image is how others see us. A distinction can be made between achieved and ascribed identity. Achieved identity is determined by what one does, while ascribed identity derives from fixed expectations based on non-chosen characteristics such as sexual orientation, nationality, the colour of your skin, and age. According to de Mooij, the ascribed identity, defined by these fixed characteristics, is stronger in cultures with a high hierarchy, where social positions are clearly defined, than in low-hierarchy cultures, where the roles that define people's status are less important. Products — and other tangible and observable means — contribute greatly to our achieved identities. Especially in societies where the hierarchy is low and positions are not clearly defined, products have a mediating role in the development of these achieved identities. They tell us who we are, what we believe, our value systems, and our social and economic status, and illustrate the division

Blending protection with identity. Eighty-nine percent of smartphone users say they buy cases to protect the device. According to a study, 86 percent of women judge dates with a cracked phone screen negatively. Yet no one buying a well-designed, expensive status symbol would normally consider hiding it in a protective layer of rubber or leather. For a lot of people, the slim-design phone is an extension of themselves, even to the point of associating its measurements with their idealised physique.

There was a time when simply having a smartphone was a sure sign of disposable income, but no longer. There are currently more smartphones in the US than there are people.

of power. But that of course depends on the context, and the meaning can change quickly. Think, for example, of a specific brand of electric car. For one person, it could represent awareness about the environment; for another, it could represent being rich and trendy. Section 2 will elaborate further on the concept of *cultural* identity.

Globalisation - For various reasons, voluntarily or otherwise, increasingly more people move to and live in different places around the world. The general question 'Where are you from?' – or in other words, 'What is your culture?' – in an international context usually points towards a country. But what if the place in which your parents grew up is not the one where you were raised, or if that country changed dramatically after they had left? What then does the question mean in an international context?

In her TED Talk 'Don't ask me where I am from, ask me where I am a local', Taiye Selasi explains the difficulty she has with the question 'Where are you from?'. Taiye was born in England and grew up in the United States of America. Her mother – born in England and raised in Nigeria – lives in Ghana. Her father was born in the Gold Coast, a British colony, and raised in Ghana, and has lived for over 30 years in the Kingdom of Saudi Arabia. And Taiye has lived in New York, Accra, and Rome. For that reason, she wonders: 'What are we really seeking when we ask where someone comes from? And what are we really seeing when we hear an answer?' Taiye's answer is summarised in the three Rs: Rituals, Relationships, and Restraints. She stated that if we want to know each other, we should focus on these three Rs, which are our local experiences constituted in our daily Rituals;

the Relationships that shape our days; and the way we feel Restrained by the local situations in which we participate. In a globalising world, a growing number of people live significant parts of their lives in different places. Their personal stories about these Rs together shape the answer that might make more sense than a story about the place where they were born.

Bound to one place: For some people, questions such as 'Where are you from?' and 'What is your culture?' do make sense. The answers may even form an important part of their identity. However, the majority of the world's population is bound to one place, as their economic situation does not allow them to move around the world. Much more than people living in highly individualised and rich societies, people living with few resources are highly dependent on the culture they have been born into. In fact, a large group of people with a reasonable income also stay in the same place throughout their lives. The culture they live in does to a certain extent define who they are, probably a great deal more than for people who consider themselves to be global citizens, living within their own 'bubbles' and moving around easily within various cultural groups. That does not mean that people tied to one place would not be exposed to cultural variation. Different cultural groups also exist even within one location and can be identified by their specific practices. Some of these cultural groups are more open and comfortable living next to different groups, while others are more closed and may have difficulties in adapting to other cultures. If needed, could designers play a role in bridging such groups?

Third-culture kids: Since the 1950s, and introduced by John and Ruth Useem, there has been a term — Third-culture kids (TCKs) — for people who grew up in different places in the world. TCKs are people raised in a culture other than that of their parents. The 'third culture' is influenced both by their parents' culture and the culture in which they, the children, are being raised, and therefore being exposed to a greater variety of cultural influences (*John and Ruth Useem 1976*). On the one hand, TCKs are usually characterised by their mastering of at least two languages and having a great capacity to adapt to different situations or new beginnings. On the other hand, they have experienced perhaps several culture shocks during their childhood, which may have resulted in adaptation difficulties or even suffering from racism. Owing to globalisation and the growing number of TKCs in developed countries, TCKs are sometimes considered to be the 'kids of the future'.

Some people who see themselves as a TCK look to the former American President, Barack Obama, as their role model. Obama was born in Hawaii, and as a child he was raised for a few years in Indonesia. He also lived for a year of his childhood in the State of Washington and then an additional four years in Indonesia. His mother grew up in Kansas (USA) and his father in Kenya. A quality attributed to TCKs is their sensitivity as regards diversity and therefore an ability to build bridges between different cultural groups. Moreover, because of their multicultural background, people from more than one culture can relate to them.

Fish bowls and culture shocks: Especially if you are lucky enough to be able to leap out of your 'fish bowl' — namely, your own culture, the cultural group you are familiar

The startling amount of time spent online and underground by the millions of commuters who daily populate the subways of our metropoles is mind-boggling. You can argue that there is not much else to do on these long underground journeys that visual artist Jacqueline Hassink documented for her project 'iPortrait' in 2018. The mirroring effect of such extensive disconnectedness from real life magnified and in your face does conjure up some unease about our daily digital consumption.

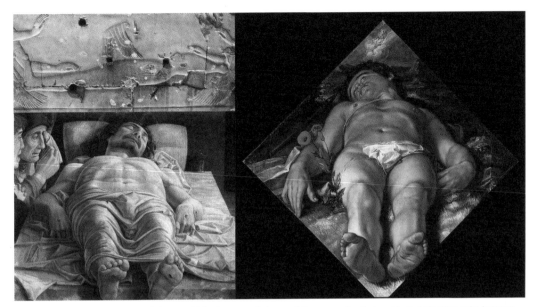

Christianity has its origins in Judaism, a Middle Eastern religion, so it is no surprise that residual similarities exist between Christian theological thought and ancient Middle Eastern religions in general. The Akkadian cult of God's son and saviour Tammuz goes back to around 3000 BC. Anthropologists claim this is an example of the archetype of a 'dying-and-rising god' found in all cultures. Other examples are the Egyptian god Osiris or the Roman god Adonis depicted above. They calmed both the fear of dying and the fear of crop failure, which are really the same fear, because crop failure leads to hunger, famine, and death.

Most religious art is allusive, or built around themes familiar to the intended observer. For the benefit of the illiterate, an elaborate iconographic system developed to conclusively identify scenes. Pictured on this spread are: Descent from the Cross by Paul Rubens, The Dead Christ and Three Mourners by Andrea Mantegna, Dying Adonis by Hendrick Goltzius 1906, and a tombstone depicting the Egyptian god Osiris.

with – and start living in another culture – you will find that there was indeed something that you could experience as 'my culture'. You begin to realise that there are aspects of your own culture, such as food, habits, products, conversations, rituals and so on, that you miss, that appeared to be important to you. Within that culture, you had different roles, and these roles now call for slightly different types of behaviour, language (think of dialects and slang), products, and so on. Now is your chance to become culture sensitive. You start to recognise what is below the surface as well as your basic assumptions on how to deal with other people, and the norms and values that you embody and convey.

At the same time, it is possible that you experience culture shock, a disorientation that occurs because of the unfamiliar ways of dealing with other people. Culture shock can be described as having four distinct phases, and will be explained further in Section 2.

Stories and myths: When somebody asks you about your culture, you will probably tell them a story. We all tell and live our stories. With stories, we reflect on and summarise our lives in terms of the people, activities, and contexts that are or were most important to us. Stories help us to deal with the complexity of our world; they somehow structure our thoughts and give us a sense of belonging. So we create stories about who we are, and these stories are based on experiences gained throughout our lives. There are long and short stories, local and master stories (or narratives), personal and collective stories. 'My culture' is the personal story that you create yourself. It does not need to be true. In fact, it cannot be an *objective* true story, because it will always be an interpretation of your personal experiences, and will be influenced by the *context* of the story (the place, the time, and the people you are or were with).

The Spanish Golden Age of baroque is full of over-decorated architecture and incomprehensible literature. This coincided with the Imperial time, the discovery of America, and the Inquisition. The moral code was highly established and controlled by the state and the church in their most hierarchical display. It defines a historic period in which the form, the style, and the meaning of art is opposed to the simplicity looked for by modernist artists like Le Corbousier, who in 1954 designed the Chapelle Notre Dame du Haut, shown above.

In Thomas Mann's novel 'Death in Venice', a great writer is experiencing a change in his conception of beauty. Mann raises a very interesting question. Is the artistic style and form linked to morality? If art is simple in its forms, will this in turn signify a morally simplistic view of the world and of human psychology, and thus also a resurgence of energies that are evil, forbidden, or even morally impossible?'

The stories that we generate about ourselves, about our culture, and about other cultures are therefore often called *myths*. A myth can be defined as any invented story, idea, or concept, and usually it is based on apparently historical events. Apparently because the events are framed in a certain way and could have been told in a different way. The myth serves to unfold part of the worldview of people or to explain a practice, belief, or natural phenomenon. The word 'myth' comes from the ancient Greek word meaning 'story' or 'plot', and the myth about a culture is the story that somehow binds a group of people together. In that sense, the myths support the commonalities between individuals. The shared stories help us to experience a feeling of belonging. Currently, the term 'myth' is often used in a negative way to indicate stories that are not scientifically true, but we should neither forget nor underestimate the positive role of myths in the past and even in today's societies. Designers can design in a way that facilitates this storytelling. Applications such as Facebook, WhatsApp, and Instagram are actually examples of storytelling spaces: platforms that support sharing interactive stories that at some point acquire cultural significance. In Section 3, you will find various ways to collect stories from intended users, and that help to build up an understanding of people's personal as well as their cultural context.

Your design culture

'Your design culture' refers to the group of designers with whom you feel affiliated. You may share with these designers similar visions and beliefs about what constitutes good and bad design. Or perhaps you are working in a similar domain, on similar projects, such as games, healthcare, or automotive. Your design culture can also be defined by the expertise that you are developing: for example, concept design, technical detailing, graphic communication, and the models and methods you use. Key is that you share values and practices with other designers. Together, you form a design culture.

Designers throughout history have formed various movements, such as Arts and Crafts (1850-1915), Art Nouveau (1880-1910), Art Deco (1910-1940), Bauhaus (1920-1934), Memphis (1981-1988), Pop Art (1958-1972), and more. And from 1978 up until the present, design historians still use the term Postmodernism to typify the design culture we are in at present. In each movement, the affiliated designers share specific

41

Social Media are trending in defining online identities. A world with no corners in which to hide, and where the use of visual imagery, spectacle, and performance has become increasingly important. It has been called the contemporary panopticon; a type of institutional building that allows all prisoners to be observed by a single security guard, without the inmates being aware they are being watched. Apple's headquarters facilitates another digital culture named holacracy. A 'complete system for self-organisation' that replaces traditional hierarchies with a supposedly more efficient system of autonomous teams of employees called 'circles'.

Almost every region across the globe wants to be 'the next Silicon Valley'. It is the people who are the drive behind the Silicon Valley IT companies. A large percentage of the general Valley population has at least an undergraduate university degree. These high-tech companies attract talent from around the world, and this diversity has led to a remarkable cross-pollination of cultural influences and ideas.

values and beliefs, and are identified by similarities in their work, in their designs. It is easier to distinguish cultural groups by looking at them in the context of the past than it is to differentiate between specific groups in the present. Consequently, the question as to which design culture you belong to right now is a difficult one. You may even think to yourself 'I am an individual designer, not part of any movement; I'm simply following my own beliefs and preferences'. And yes, it is important to some extent to follow your personal motivations. But at the same time — whether you like it or not — you will be influenced by the culture you are in at the moment and by the cultures and events that you experienced in the past.

Mapping your design culture: A way to determine in which design culture you participate is by mapping factors. The main question is: With which group of designers do you feel affiliated? The first layer presents the designer as an *individual* person, with a vision as to what design is, should be, and can do; with beliefs about what is a good design; and with personal interests, possibilities, and limitations in the designing. The second layer is *contextual*: for example, the design context you are in, the design school, the company, the location, the country, and the society. For instance, the economic and political situation as well as the technological possibilities will influence your personal perspective. Your historical background forms the third layer. It includes the generation you grew up with, the culture of the design school in which you were educated, the places you lived, and all of your life experiences; each of these factors somehow contributes to your design culture. These layers can be used to map the factors that are important for you as a designer. Then, in a second step, you map designers that are similar to your profile. They are somehow connected and form a network. In the longer term, these networks can be recognised as specific design cultures, and feature outstanding designers and design researchers who endorse a philosophy about what effect the design should have.

HCD, UX designer, Service designer ... , the list of descriptive terms to typify designers is growing. With which one do you feel connected or which one would you add? There is a lot of overlap between the terms, and one does not necessarily exclude the other.

Since the industrial revolution, industrial design has become a profession with certain designs and innovations becoming so successful that some designers, predominantly white men who helped shaping the profession, have become international celebrities. Designer Viktor Papanek criticised his profecssion in his book 'Design for the Real World' (1974) with a statement directed at designers who fail to take their responsibility towards society: 'There must be professions more harmful than industrial design, but not many'.

How culture sensitive are you?

'If you go through life convinced that your way is always best, all the new ideas in the world will pass you by.'
(Akio Morita, designer and founder of Sony)

Now that you have been introduced to the world of culture sensitivity, you can finish reading this part of the book with questions designed to help you reflect on your own culture sensitivity. Ask yourself these questions now as well as during each phase of a design project; they will help you to remain perceptive and empathetic in relation to the cultural context of the design.

Do you know your perspective? In which cultural 'bubble' do you live? Are you aware of your own culture and the effects it has on how you act and think? How do cultural aspects like the political situation in your country, your upbringing, or your daily routines influence what you assume to be appropriate for a design, or – even more important – what the effect of your design will be on people and societies? Knowing where you are coming from helps you to understand and define where you are going and what you want people to accomplish with your designs. If you develop your personal viewpoint, your stance, you will have a solid basis on which to understand and work with other people's values. If you are lucky, you will be able to 'leap out of your fishbowl' and gain insight into your own cultural values.

Do you recognise and acknowledge your blind spots? Do you recognise your own limitations? The term blind spots refers here to *'the things that you do not know that you do not know'*. There are things that we know that we do not know. For instance, I know that I do not know much about the importance of hierarchy in co-creation sessions, or the meaning of a racing bike in the south of France. Since I know that I do not know this,

Millions of people worldwide still have to live under shocking conditions in places like the slum in Mumbai, India above, that define a part of our global culture. Peoples fate is largely defined by the place they were born. Yet all people in the world today may on many levels have more in common with each other then they have with their grandparents, who grew up in a totaly different world and a totaly different reality defined by long vanished cultural references en codes.

A culture shock is the personal disorientation a person may feel when experiencing an unfamiliar way of life due to immigration or a visit to a new country, a move between social environments, or simply a transition to another lifestyle.

I can decide to search for answers. But for my *blind spots* this is not possible, because I just do not know what I should know. Therefore, we first need to be aware and certain that blind spots exist, that our individual chasms might be close by. Cultural theories and examples from real life help to become sensitive in relation to where the blind spots may pop up. Therefore, try to have an open attitude; this will enable you to gain insights you would never have thought possible because they might not be relevant or even exist in your own culture.

Do you anticipate culture shocks? Have you ever experienced culture shock? What did you feel, and how did you deal with it? When you dive into a new culture – for example, when doing design research in the field – but also when doing desktop research, be aware of the feelings and thoughts you experience. At first, it might feel exciting and inspiring, because everything is new and usually designers like that, right? But after a while, when confronted with norms and values that are not your own, you may feel irritated or even disoriented. Questions such as 'Am I going to adapt to the culture or to what extent do I follow my own?' Or 'What actually are my own values and practices? I was not aware of them'. And most of all, 'Which values are really important to me and will steer my design direction?'

Do you consider the effect of your design on cultures? What future do you envision? How will people live together? Products do influence people's lives; for example, the introduction of the smartphone made it easy to make ad hoc appointments and to stay connected every moment of the day. In high economic cultures, children at an early age are already able to use a mobile phone, which is helpful for parents.

Because members of a Western culture spend much of their free time in front of the television or movie screen, celebrity endorsements are paramount to a brand's success. If pop stars like Kylie Jenner Balmain and popular sportsmen like LeBron James endorse a specific brand of headphones, we assume that must mean something.

By the end of the 1940s, there was a burgeoning awareness that a brand was not just a mascot, a catchphrase, or a company's product label: the company as a whole should have an identity or a corporate consciousness. This endeavour led to an examination of what brands mean to the culture and to people's lives. A range of consumer-celebrity relationships conspired to allow consumers to develop a portfolio of relationships that function as creators of meaning.[5]

This possibility influences the perception of time and safety. What if the child does not respond to its parents' messages within an hour? How would that make the parents feel? It is not simply the individual parent who will change his or her attitude towards time and safety. Influenced by each other's behaviour, we collectively change our culture.

Do you embrace the need for identity? How do you identify people and through what kind of expressions? And how do you express who you are? In today's rapidly globalising world, there are products and services that are designed to be 'timeless', such as smartphones, computers, and furniture (e.g. Ikea). Details that could be culture specific, with function and form details that are typical and refer to a specific place, are avoided. An advantage for companies is that if they want to sell worldwide and in large numbers, the production can be standardised. A disadvantage is that they do not connect with local cultures that have developed over time. A shared history, together with the associated manifestations, gives people a cultural identity and, as a result, a sense of belonging.

In closing Now that we have explored our 'own perspective', and have a better understanding of our culture and what we mean by culture sensitivity, we can go into depth. The following section discusses in more detail those aspects that are important in understanding cultures. How can we view and identify other cultures? And what happens when cultures come together? These aspects not only offer starting points for design projects but are also valuable in terms of taking into account projects that do not focus primarily on culture.

A LENS FOR VIEWING

CULTURE
DEFINED

Culture can be looked at from various perspectives: for example, how
do designers view culture, and what principles should be considered
in your designs? In addition, how can we look at culture without
remaining superficial? To give depth to the term 'culture', several
aspects are highlighted that will help you to view, understand, give
meaning to, and communicate about culture in multiple ways. The
distinctions discussed in this part offer a language in which to talk
about culture and the means to design with it.

Karl Benz invented the first car in 1885. The Electric Construction Corporation produced the first electric cars in 1888. The 'Car of Tomorrow' is a product of its times. The Mercedes-Benz Vision AVTR concept vehicle presented in 2020 features 33 'bionic flaps' on the back, designed to facilitate communication with the driver and the outside world. Despite its futuristic design, it still echoes both the conventional petrol car and futurism from the past, like the Norman Bell Geddes aerodynamic Teardrop car from 1933.

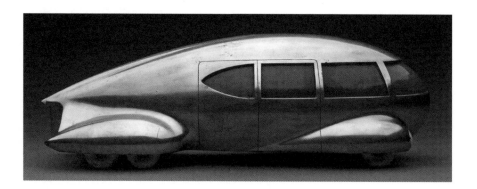

STARTING POINTS

This part begins with a section on diverse lenses designed to examine culture, and it concludes with a lens meaningful for designers. The design discipline borrows and adopts theories and methods from various other disciplines. A few that are relevant for culture-sensitive design are mentioned here.

In the words of Einstein, 'The true sign of intelligence is not knowledge but imagination'. We cannot solve our problems with the same thinking we used when we created them. No problem can be solved from the same level of consciousness that created it. The only real valuable thing is institution. Design is about creation, while other sciences deal with what already exists.[6]

Most disciplines approach culture in a holistic way, striving to study the 'big picture' and the total collective representations associated with a particular society *(Hellemans, 2014)*. Ideally, designers implement an integral approach that zooms both in and out. From the zooming out perspective, the bigger picture is seen in such a way that the effect of the design on people's lives can be estimated. Basically, designers are oriented towards the future.

From a historical perspective, culture in design is obviously studied on the basis of what we know from the past: for example, how products and other artefacts obtained their meaning over time. Design historians such as Paul du Gay and Edward Miller study material culture, the meaning of things and how it evolves, and the role of designers who co-produce or create meaning through things. In *The Story of the Sony Walkman* (1997), du Gay and his co-authors describe in the Circuit of Culture five processes that influence the socio-cultural meaning of things in different societies. Section 3 explains this model and how designers can use it.

Historians describe design education movements such as Bauhaus, and they identify and indicate the meaning of design styles such as Art Deco, Constructivism, and Postmodernism. Or they interpret the work of individuals who have criticised the role of design in society, such as Viktor Papanek with his *Design for the Real World* (1971). Understanding these cultural developments will facilitate a better understanding of the influence of design in the present as well as a deeper insight into what the meaning of design could or should be in the future. However, designers are often not interested in history. As design historian Timo de Rijk states: 'The discourse of design – and product design in particular – is hardly based on history. This is mainly because design should be future oriented, a notion that is heavily at odds with the development of a history that can be actively utilized' (de Rijk, 2014, p.II). And indeed, there is only a future when we assume a past, and there are good reasons that historical knowledge matters for designers: for example, if you design because you want to bring about a change for the better – which is an important motivation for many designers – then you need to know the history of people as well as the problems you would like to solve. A change for the better presumes a past that was not good enough – but for what reasons? We run the risk of throwing the baby out with the bath water if we first do not understand the past.

Another reason to study the past is that new designs need to be understood. New ideas for the future need to link somehow with how people perceive their world, and with how they communicate and deal with each other. These ways of dealing with each other can be understood from developments over time. Historical knowledge also helps you to shake off what exists in the present. It may not help you so much to really *predict* the future, but at least it will free you from the past and help you to see

At the turn of the 20th century, the horse was still the primary means of transportation. As Americans became more prosperous, they turned to the newly invented motor vehicle. Owing to habits and conventions, these were designed to look like motorised bicycles or traditional carriages without horses. The image left shows the original Benz Patent-Motorwagen, first built in 1885. On the right the electric car, built by Thomas Parker, photographed in 1895.

Initially, cars were electric: safe, easy to handle, and clean. Gasoline cars were noisy, needed a hand crank to start, required changing gears, and their exhaust pipe fumes were unpleasant. Then Henry Ford's mass-produced Model T came along, combined with the discovery of Texas crude oil that made gas inexpensive and readily available for rural Americans, very few of whom had electricity at that time. Filling stations began to pop up across the country.

a new, alternative possibility (Harari, 2015, p.77). Perhaps it is typical of designers that they have no trouble shedding the past. But even if you want to break away from it, it is useful to begin with an understanding of the past, because it can serve as a rich source of inspiration. Insights gleaned from the past can spark your creativity and give you a solid, substantiated basis for the development of your own point of view about your desired or intended design result.

Culture and design can also be viewed from an anthropological perspective. Here, people — in all their facets, behaviour, and societies — are central to this discipline. Culture is studied to understand the meaning of people's daily practices in relationship to the designed environment. How and why do people live and cooperate with each other? What are the — often hidden — social symbols and rules, and how do they change over time? One of the most famous cultural anthropologists, often mentioned as one of the founders of the discipline, is Clifford Geertz. He perceived culture as being a set of control mechanisms (plans, recipes, rules, and instructions) for regulating human behaviour in a specific context. For his ethnographic studies, he used the term 'thick description', emphasising that human behaviour should be understood in its cultural context and at a certain time and place. *(Clifford Geertz, 1973)*

Likewise, Edward Hall, a well-known anthropologist, is famous for his *proxemics theory* about different preferences of physical distance between people, and for his theory about *contextual communication* that distinguishes low- and high-context cultures.

Similar to design historians, the work of anthropologists aims to examine cultures that are by default rooted in the past and occur in the present. Anthropological studies, such as ethnographic research, focus on current cultural practices. In contrast, designers look at the same practices, but are focused more on changes for the future. 'As creators of models, prototypes and propositions, designers occupy a dialectical space between the world that is and the world that could be. Informed by the past and the present, their activity is oriented towards the future' *(Margolin, 2007, p.4)*. In a comparison of design and anthropology, Otto and Smith (2013) state: 'Although anthropology has an interest in social change and people's imaginations of the future, as a discipline it lacks tools and practices to actively engage and collaborate in people's formation of their futures *(p.3)*'. In a comparison of design and anthropology, Ton Otto

Yuchen Cai, 23, a graduate of Shanghai Jiao Tong University, created The Float as her vision to provide mobility for a world where autonomy is the norm. It makes use of magnetic-levitation technology and a tessellated design. It has pods for either one or two people, and numerous pods can be attached via a magnetic belt. Connected pods can change the opacity of the glass for privacy or social interaction. It includes a smartphone app that allows users to hire The Float at the touch of a button.

Six reasons designers should study history: to avoid roads already taken and that led to undesirable situations; to avoid the risk of losing something valuable, akin to throwing the baby out with the bath water; to make sure new ideas are understood in terms of the language of the past (the history of the present); to free themselves from the past; to inspire, to spark new thoughts, to make novel combinations that lead to new ideas; and to know their own stance: namely, where they come from and where they are going.

writes: 'Designing and planning for change involves the simultaneous conceptualisation of a past that makes the desired future possible'. In other words, designers need to understand past and present cultures in order to design a possible future that is also desirable. This is the point at which both disciplines meet and can benefit from each other. Companies nowadays recognise the added value of collaborations with anthropologists and designers in the field of product innovation.

Another perspective on cultural studies is that of cross-cultural management and communication. The goal and interest of these studies is to improve the effectiveness and efficiency of cross-cultural collaborations in the context of businesses and other organisations such as hospitals, educational institutes, and others. The aim is to support the relationship between people from different cultural backgrounds. Barriers in cross-cultural collaborations arise because people have learned different ways of dealing with each other. They use different social codes that are communicated through language, gestures, division of roles, and so on. Several researchers have developed sets of dimensions along which cultures (grouped by nation) can be measured. Their theories are used in cultural studies and training programmes all over the world. Although reducing culture to a set of dimensions has often been criticised, they can be very helpful if used wisely, as is shown later in this section. *(Hofstede, Hofstede, and Minkov, 2010; Trompenaars and Hampden Turner, 1998; House et al. 2004; Honold, 2004; Meyer, 2015).*

The concept of culture in design can also be approached from a philosophical perspective in which scientists analyse, for example, the impact of technology and design on individual lives and on society as a whole, taking into account ethical consequences. An example of a philosopher who is cited regularly in design studies is Bruno Latour. Educated as a philosopher and cultural anthropologist, Latour explores the relationships between science, technology, and society. He is known for his concept of '*script*', describing the *mediation* of action by products; like the script of a film or a theatrical production, artefacts *prescribe* – and by doing so *mediate* – how people use them and consequently behave *(Latour, 1992)*. Inspired by his work, the Dutch philosopher Peter Paul Verbeek states that designers *create morality*. Therefore, how we think about what is 'good' and 'bad' and act upon these values is influenced by our designed

51

Most Western cultures are built around ideals of individual choice and personal identity. But the need to belong, to be approved or appreciated by our peers is among the highest human motivations, which allows social media to enter our lives while pulling the strings. The film 'Pinocchio' by Matteo Garrone is based on the 1883 children's novel by Carlo Collodi. It is about a mischievous wooden puppet that disobeys its creator, and is notably characterised by its frequent tendency to cheat and lie, which causes its nose to grow.

Given a selection of choices, people rarely ask what is not on the list, why they are given these options and not others, and what are the provider's goals. There is no questioning as to whether the choices empower the original need or are actually a distraction. 'It is easier to fool people than to convince them that they have been fooled.'[7]

environment. This means that what you have designed — whether a product or a service — also raises an immediate moral question. Is what we do with the design good or bad? Verbeek uses obstetric ultrasound as an example. He describes how ultrasound technology mediates in how parents experience their unborn child, and what moral questions arise from this technology. The fact that parents can see their foetus in real-life size, for instance, and separate from the mother, makes this unborn baby an independent human being. And this raises the question about who is responsible for his or her life. Does this unborn baby have an individual right to live, regardless of whether it is a boy or a girl, or is physically or potentially mentally handicapped? The device could be used for purposes of gender selection, especially in a culture where women and men do not have equal rights. What if the design also included a possible future scenario involving the unborn baby, depicting a grown-up, independent woman taking financial care of her family? Parents might then think differently about this unborn baby and make other decisions. Whatever we design raises the question of how we relate to each other and how products mediate in this. The outcomes are highly influenced by culture *(Razzaghi et al., 2009)*.

And then there is the cultural perspective of the design discipline itself. Because of their future-oriented approach, designers seem to overlook valuable elements that can be learned from history. However, the perspective of the design historian as well as that of other disciplines engaged in studying culture do not fully align with the interests of designers and the work they do. Therefore, designers need to have some sort of tools or guidelines to support them in examining culture in such a way that it fits the future-oriented perspective of the design discipline, incorporating what can be learned from both the past and the present. Theory and models should be in tune with designers'

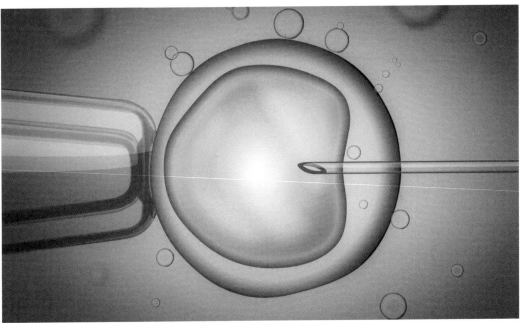

Obstetric ultrasound raises the moral question of whether the design should be implemented in a way that prevents rather than protects gender selection. The use of pre-implantation genetic diagnosis technology may help to prevent hereditary diseases. But concerns have been raised that this could be translated into using the technology for cosmetic purposes and the enhancement of human traits, with far-reaching implications for the greater society.

mind-sets, which can shift from products to people or from functions to values, as is depicted in the reasoning model explained later in this section. Values can be universal but also specific to a culture. When these values are fully understood, functions can be defined; in turn, by looking at the functions of products, the underlying cultural values can be discerned.

In the present book, models and methods for analysing cultures from different disciplines are presented in such a way that they will be helpful for designers. People with a mind-set that has been defined in other disciplines – another subculture, so to say – may frame the concept of culture differently.

Approaching culture: five principles - Five basic principles are important with relation to use of the term culture. Because the concept of culture is approached from different perspectives, and can raise many discussions, these principles are highlighted.

▶ *Cultures change over time:* If we look at the surface, it might be apparent that cultures do change. New subcultures arrive and others go. Pushed frequently by commerce, new forms of food, fashion, cars, and furniture are introduced and feed into the creation of subcultures, such as Hipsters and Rockabillies. These kinds of changes seem to occur increasingly faster under the influence of the Internet and other communication technology. New technologies lead to new products and services that change our behaviour; the mobile phone, for example, changed the meaning of time. In wealthy countries, the habit was to plan trips or vacations far in advance. And when travelling abroad, even for a long period, it was acceptable to have no contact with family or friends at home. Nowadays, however, appointments are made ad hoc and at short notice, and parents

Japan has the unfortunate reputation of being one of the worlds most stereotyped country. To assume all Japanese love animegao kigurumi – a type of cosplay using masks and costumes to portray anime or game characters in the real world – is like assuming all Americans love baseball and handguns. The Korean Wave (Hallyu, a Chinese term) is one of the most modern sub-cultures, originating in South Korea and highly popular in Russia. It consists of fans of Korean music groups (K-POP). Hallyu also involves a passion for cooking, video games, movies, and the language of South Korea.

Western classical music was not introduced to the Chinese public until Christian missionaries arrived in the 19th century, after which it quickly gained popularity and prestige as a symbol of the Western culture of scientific progress and modernisation. Today some 36 million Chinese children are studying the piano. The future of Western classical music as a 'living art form may be in the hands of the East's rising musicians rather than those of the West, where classical music is marginalised by the contemporary entertainment industry as an esoteric genre for a privileged few.' [8]

track the travel movements of their children constantly. If we typify a culture or a cultural group, we always need to be aware that it is a blueprint of the *current* situation, and it does not necessarily say anything about the future. At the same time, when looking at a deeper level of the underlying values that a group of people share and that are based on a long history, things might need to be done quite differently. For designers — who are by default involved in a process of change — it is important to be conscious of the dynamic nature of cultures and what that implies.

▸ *Cultures are examined in context:* Context is defined as the situation within which something exists or happens, and that can help explain it. It is situated in a *place* and at a certain *time*. The factors that describe a context can be physical and concrete, such as climate and the things that people possess; it can also be non-physical and abstract, such as political issues and religious beliefs. Factors can also develop in virtual space and time (i.e. on the Internet). To apply a culture-sensitive approach, and to avoid generalisations, designers should describe explicitly the context for which they design, such as 'design for the elderly' (i.e. which elderly, where, and when?). It is crucial to delineate the cultural context; though difficult, it is a key element, because where does the targeted context begin and end? Products — even services — flow; they are not bound to a fixed place, but the people who will use them are more or less bound to a location. Designers benefit from this delineation; a client's brief, for example, that states 'design for Western European women' will not help you to imagine possible situations. Within Western Europe there are many subcultures. If you do not take these into consideration, your design may not only become superficial but you will also run the risk of overlooking insights that are important for your design. Furthermore, it is necessary to specify the period of time. The Western European culture now differs considerably from the one that existed 20 years ago, and certainly differs from the culture that lies 20 years ahead. Therefore, you need to be specific about where and when your design will intervene.

▸ *Individual people do not represent a culture:* Individuals often feel stereotyped if other people apply to them the *types* of the group they live in. This might be a sensitive matter, especially in highly individualised societies. People feel put into boxes, and these boxes do not do justice to these individuals' personality, and it feels to them as

A popular stereotype is the film cowboy who personifies a national myth of the USA: a courageous man with a horse and a gun, waging a personal battle against injustice in a lawless and corrupt world. This myth disguises a short and violent colonialisation period, better typified by another symbol: the devil's rope, better known as the American invention of barbed wire in 1873 by John Barn Gates and patented and sold by Joseph Glidden. It was used predominantly to keep people locked out or in. The wall of crosses in Heroica Nogales, Mexico, is adorned with the names of those who have died crossing the USA border.

In 1862, President Abraham Lincoln had signed the Homestead Act which specified that any honest citizen could lay claim to up to 160 acres (0.6 sq km) of land in America's western territories. Barbed wire changed what the Homestead Act could not. it was ruthlessly and cynically deployed by those who argued that Native Americans didn't really have a right to their own territory, because they weren't eveloping it in the style that Europeans saw fit.

though this stereotyping limits their freedom to choose the boxes. But an individual person does not necessarily represent a culture. In other words, characteristics of a cultural group cannot be applied one-to-one to an individual person and vice versa. A culture is composed of various individuals that are not necessarily the same but together they form a group. Culture is like a forest; the trees together form a specific type of forest (e.g. a tropical forest), but the single trees are not all the same (e.g. palm trees); they differ, and, on their own, they do not represent the forest, but they do need each other to survive.

▶ *Personal and cultural values and practices are intertwined:* It is difficult to distinguish which individual values and practices are based typically on personal, inherited traits and which ones are learned through the culture to which a person feels he or she belongs. Those who leap out of their own fishbowl (cultural bubble) are fortunate that they are able to reflect on their personality (their beliefs, values, and practices) and experience how culture plays a role in their lives.

User Experience design researchers currently study people's individual needs and dreams. But to what extent are these needs and dreams influenced by the cultures the people are in? Many of these needs are influenced by what others think and do, about what is needed to deal with each other socially and culturally. It is important to take into account both the individual and the cultural perspective. The one cannot do without the other.

▶ *Designers influence cultures through design:* Products and services influence people's lives. The designer's challenge is to find out how. Designers may offer people new utilitarian functions, such as mobile communication or quick and comfortable ways

The US$121,280 Caviar iPhone 11 Pro Solarius Zenith is a design accessory that 'only the worthy' can hold in their hands. As William James wrote in 1890: 'A man's self is the sum total of all that he can call his, not only his body and his psychic powers, but his clothes and his house, his wife and children, his ancestors and friends, his reputation and works, his lands and horses, and yacht and bank-account.'

to commute; in the meantime, however, they also challenge people's socio-cultural values, such as social status in the group, individual freedom, and perception of time. The designer's solution may address values that are different from those that are not yet acceptable to the cultural group, but which over time will change people's lives. It is important to take into consideration how a design can change these patterns as well as whether or not that is the desired outcome.

How can we view culture?

As we have already seen, culture can be studied from different perspectives in different disciplines. This section proposes a lens through which a designer can look at culture. With this proposed lens, we begin with relationships between people, and with how they interact with each other in a specific group and context. The starting point is that the designed world – products and services or other manifestations of our designed world – are mediators in these relationships.

Values and practices People share certain values. These values can only be observed and experienced by means of what people say and do, and in relation to the things that surround them. We call the expressions of these values *practices*.

In certain past East Asian cultures, pearls and jade were major status symbols, reserved exclusively for royalty. Similar legal exclusions applied to the toga and its variants in ancient Rome, and to cotton in the Aztec Empire. Special colours such as imperial yellow (in China) or royal purple (in ancient Rome) were reserved for royalty, with severe penalties for unauthorised displays.

Values: a difficult term that needs explanation - To begin with, let us have a look at the reasoning model of Norbert Roozenburg and Johannes Eekels, an abstract representation of how designers reason along the line of values, needs, functions, and properties towards their final form, and vice versa *(van Boeijen, Daalhuizen, Zijlstra (Eds.), 2020)*. The arrows indicate causal relations in *analysing* from *form to values* and *synthesising*, which goes in the opposite direction, from *value to form*. This model helps to indicate where and how cultural values are linked to aspects that need to be considered. The focus here is on *cultural* values. In the multidisciplinary context in which designers work, it can be confusing to talk about values, because the term is used differently across disciplines. While *value* can be understood as the underlying reason for our practices (including things), the term *values* can be used to refer to the moral evaluation of our practices (are they considered good or bad, right or wrong). Prasad Boradkar gives a useful overview of different value types. It shows a list of these value types with an example of how a bicycle is evaluated from, among others, a utilitarian, an economic, and an environmental perspective. *(Prasad Boradkar, 2010)* Of course, you can only evaluate the value or cultural value and meaning of this bicycle if you know the specific context: when, where, and in which situation the bicycle is used. Therefore, it is important to know the *context* when talking about values.

Take the example of the syringe. What situation or context do you imagine when looking at the syringe? What is the value of this product? The mother and child may illustrate the context that you imagined. But the value of the syringe changes completely when pictured as a part of the world of heroin addicts. This awareness of different meanings in different contexts is useful for design, because rethinking them can help to align a product with various possible contexts and/ or lead to new product ideas, such as the low-cost, single-use syringe designed to prevent infections. In my work, I often see designers starting from a kind of global perspective with design briefs that are very broadly formulated, such as 'designing for Western European women'. This makes sense if the company is aiming for large-scale production, but from a design perspective it is not always fruitful. A more specific understanding of the different contexts can lead to interesting and meaningful ideas.

Kitsch is a modern phenomenon, coinciding with social changes such as mass production, plastics, television, the rise of the middle class, and public education – all of which have factored in a perception of oversaturation of art produced for the popular taste. Las Vegas is its capital, and Liberace was its king. The extravagant piano player is known less for the music he made than for his $300,000, 16-foot, 175-pound sequined capes. He drove his cars onto the stage, and would emerge wearing a clothing ensemble that matched the car, such as one encrusted with a mosaic of jewel-like mirrors in patterns of prancing horses.

VALUES

Utilitarian
Symbolic
Cultural
Environmental
Comfort
Innovative
Ergonomic
Economic
Aestetic
Brand
Historical
Social
Emotional
Political

Up until the 1950s, the cargo bike was mostly for professional use. It is now making a comeback in urban traffic as an efficient replacement for the car. Cargo bikes with three wheels are particularly popular, being practical, affordable, and stable, even when the bicycle is loaded with goods.

Cultural values can be defined as *collective* tendencies to prefer a certain course of events above another, expressed by qualifications such as good and bad, dirty and clean, ugly and beautiful' (Hofstede, 2005). This refers to the moral evaluation of our practices, and these can differ from group to group. In one culture, for example, it is perceived as good to ask the lecturer questions *in public*, as it means that you are interested and eager to learn. In another culture, asking a lecturer questions in public is not appreciated, because it implies that the lecturer was not clear, or that he or she might not be capable of answering the question. These values and related practices − including the products that mediate in these social relationships − are learned, not inherited, and are often passed from generation to generation. Basically, you could say that these values are there to interact with each other in an effective way.

Values are abstract; they cannot be viewed, but are observed only through the practice of them. A frequently used metaphor is that of the iceberg, as it demonstrates that a part of the culture can easily be observed while the values remain hidden. A similar way of showing that values are beneath the surface is through the metaphor of an onion: the values are hidden in the core. Another metaphor is the fishbowl. We are like a fish, not aware of the water to which we are so accustomed. In her thesis on intercultural design research, Chen Hao added the metaphor of a duck. She wrote: 'In order to connect two different cultures, a person needs to be like a duck, which knows both water and air, unlike the majority of fish or birds' *(Hao, 2019)*.

Individual, cultural, and universal human values: Why do we need these underlying values? The scientist Salomon Schwarz distinguishes six main features of human values that help us to understand what values are and why we need them (Schwarz, 2006):

The spectacle of bodyguards wearing business suits and earphones and running in unison alongside Kim Jong Un's armoured limousine on numerous high-profile occasions serves as a major propaganda tool. The image symbolises the importance of the North Korean Supreme Leader, and the power of his 100,000-man-strong personal security apparatus.

A crown is a traditional symbolic form of head adornment worn by a monarch or a deity. It represents power, legitimacy, victory, triumph, honour, and glory, and often immortality, righteousness, and resurrection. Special headgear to designate rulers dates back to pre-history, and is found in many separate civilisations around the globe.

▸ *They represent affective beliefs*: We become emotional when our values are enabled or inhibited; for example, we get angry or annoyed when someone violates our value of respect. They are 'basic assumptions' about how we should deal with each other; *(Trompenaars and Hampden Turner, 1998)*

▸ *They refer to desirable goals*: We are motivated to pursue goals that align with our values; for example, benevolence motivates us to help a friend when our assistance is needed;

▸ *They transcend specific situations*: Our values are significant for all life domains; for example, benevolence motivates us to be helpful in all life domains, such as at home or at work, for friends or for strangers;

▸ *They guide selection or evaluation of behaviour, people, and events*: Our values help us to decide what is good or bad for us;

▸ *They have a hierarchical structure*: Individuals and groups have different 'priorities', for example, the value of social status is more important to people in one context than to those in another;

▸ *Their relative importance guides action*: The trade-off among relevant, competing values guides action.

Practices: manifestations of cultural values - Only through our practices can we understand cultures. Let us take the metaphor of the onion. The onion represents cultural values as the core of a culture. They are hidden in the centre and surrounded by their related *practices* in three layers: rituals, heroes, and symbols. 'Symbols' — the outer layer that represents values — can be words, gestures, behaviour, images, objects (such as products), services, art, language and dialects, fashion, and more. For designers, this is

Sci-fi artist and body architect Lucy McRae created 'Future Day Spa', a 'personalised, guided experience, offering treatments that evoke states of love, trust, and relaxation'. The space consists of a highly sanitised room with two vacuum beds and a large vacuum chamber, ministering vacuum therapy. Materials include steel, acrylic, closed cell poly-foam, clear vinyl, and mylar. A voiceover says 'It's like being hugged by a machine'.

In many cultures, individuals are considered to be worthy of respect until they prove otherwise. Courtesies that show respect may include simple physical signs like a slight bow, a smile, direct eye contact, a simple handshake, or a hug; however, those acts may have very different interpretations, depending on the cultural context.

the most prominent layer, because it includes almost every aspect that a designer will elaborate on. Another layer is called *'heroes'*. Heroes are people in a cultural group that represent the values that are important to the group. These role models can be real or fictional, alive or dead. Nelson Mandela, for example, could represent the value of freedom. A fictional character such as Harry Potter represents care. There are also anti-heroes like Voldemort that represent evil. Design researchers can use heroes to identify the local values. Designers can use these heroes in a design project to communicate the values that are considered important. The third layer is *'rituals'*, defined as the collective activities that mark important transitions or milestones. A wedding ceremony, for instance, is a ritual during which a public commitment is made regarding the nature of a relationship, and it demarcates the start of a new situation. Often these rituals are simply present, and we do not know who their original designers were, probably because the rituals evolved over a long period of time, anonymously and in everyday life.

Rituals and routines - In the design education practice the terms 'ritual' and 'routine' are often used interchangeably. However, we see them as two distinct practices, and for the following reasons.

▸ *Routines:* are types of behaviour that are repeated regularly and tend to occur subconsciously, such as reading from left to right or from right to left. In a product-user relationship, the term refers to the actions that people perform in a specific situation at a specific time: for example, starting the day by drinking a cup of tea or coffee. In comparison to rituals, routines do not have a specific socio-cultural meaning but are based on practical conventions. Obviously, designers need to know these routines: for example, not only to attune their designs to existing routines but also to introduce

The Salvadora persica, also known as the 'toothbrush tree', provides probably the oldest tool for cleaning teeth, used by millions all over the world. A 'chewing stick' contains an antibiotic that keeps the mouth clean and also prevents toothaches. In addition, it contains active compounds that reduce decay, gum disease, and plaque. The Maasai brush for up to 10 minutes at a time. The sticks are cheap, small, and easy to transport, so are always handy when needed.

Alll societies use distictive rituals and routines for various purposes. Rites of passage, atonement and purification, oaths of allegiance, dedication ceremonies, coronations and presidential inaugurations, marriages, funerals, and more. Even common everyday actions like hand-shaking and greeting may be termed as rituals. new routines that are associated with their products. People cannot change their routines easily, so you may not want to challenge them with new behaviour. Take, for instance, the operation of a lamp's on-off switch; people in India are accustomed to flipping a button upwards to turn on a lamp, while in European countries it is the other way around. Sometimes you do want to change people's routines, however, because they are not healthy or sustainable. Persuasive design strategies are used to find solutions that transform these routines into new and better ones.

▶ *Rituals* - as defined here in the context of a cultural practice - typically have a social significance. They are developed to enhance specific social values, such as connectedness and harmony among group members. A useful definition is *a stereotyped sequence of activities performed in a specific situation in time and place, repeated over time, and designed to support shared social values.* In a product-user relationship, it refers to the actions people perform to maintain specific values. A tea ceremony, for instance, can serve to perpetuate the importance of harmony within humanity and with nature, to foster the notion of a disciplined mind and a heart in balance, and to ease the path to enlightenment. Under the influence of individualisation and secularisation, you may wonder whether such cultural rituals are still needed. However — to enhance group values — precisely through these developments there is a great need for new, contemporary forms that replace traditional rituals. The essence of a cultural ritual is that it arises from and is shaped in the culture. It cannot be imposed from the outside. Designers need a solid understanding of the social behaviors and routines that characterise both traditional rituals as the changing contemporary ones. In a study on construction work cooperation, Leonore van

The Japanese tea ceremony is a cultural activity. A wide range of tea utensils (chadōgu) in different styles and motifs are used for different events and in different seasons. All the tools are handled with exquisite care. Some items, such as the Chigusa (tea storage jar) are so revered that they can be given proper names like people. A chakai is a relatively simple course of hospitality. A chaji, the most formal gathering, can last up to four hours.

den Endel distinguishes three levels where such social rituals are practiced: at team level to build commitment and solidarity; at institutional level to create space for officials to mediate between the project and the environment and; at societal level to gain the support of citizens and other stakeholders *(van den Ende, 2016).*

Cultural dimensions A culture can be examined along specific dimensions. Several researchers have developed dimensions along which cultural value orientations are measured. The basic idea is that groups of people share certain values, and the groups are distinguished by differences in value orientation: that is, the degree of relative importance.

Dimensions for collective value orientations - Geert Hofstede developed six dimensions that typify national cultures. Along these dimensions, the dominant values – what people in general consider to be important in social interactions – were measured for a number of countries. The scores on these dimensions are used to describe national cultures and how they differ from each other. Other researchers, such as Robert House et al. (2004) in The Globe Project, Fons Trompenaars and Charles Hampden Turner (1998), and later Erin Meyer (2015), have also developed similar sets of dimensions. All these dimensions represent preferences for one state of affairs over another and that distinguish countries from each other. Because the country scores on these dimensions are relative, they are meaningfully only by comparison. One of these dimensions, for example, is power distance: the extent to which less powerful members of a society accept and expect that power is distributed unequally. For some countries,

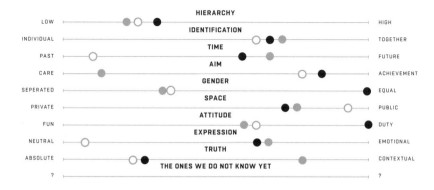

LOW		**HIERARCHY**	HIGH
INDIVIDUAL		**IDENTIFICATION**	TOGETHER
PAST		**TIME**	FUTURE
CARE		**AIM**	ACHIEVEMENT
SEPERATED		**GENDER**	EQUAL
PRIVATE		**SPACE**	PUBLIC
FUN		**ATTITUDE**	DUTY
NEUTRAL		**EXPRESSION**	EMOTIONAL
ABSOLUTE		**TRUTH**	CONTEXTUAL
?		**THE ONES WE DO NOT KNOW YET**	?

Socio-cultural dimensions can be used as a checklist for designers: what is your own preferred value orientation and what are the related practices? For the design process: What are the shared values or different value orientations among stakeholders or in the team, and how do you align your methods and tools with these? For the design itself: What values will your product support or challenge? Various sets of cultural dimensions can be applied.

Dissent is a sentiment or philosophy of non-agreement or opposition to a prevailing idea or an entity. Politically repressive regimes may prohibit any form of dissent, leading to suppression of social or political activism. Individuals who do not conform to or support the policies of certain states are known as 'dissidents'. Several thinkers have argued that a healthy society needs not only to protect but also to encourage dissent.

the measured scores on this dimension are higher than in others, which means that the general tendency is for people to accept that power in those countries is distributed more unequally than in others. These dimensions are often used to explain cultural differences in social relationships, or to prepare social encounters when, for example, cultures with different value orientations meet: for instance, in international business situations. The theory has often been criticised, however, because approaching cultures from a national perspective, and measuring and typifying cultures through numbers that are based on questionnaires and averages of large populations, do not do justice to the complexity of what culture entails. Nevertheless, despite the critique – and provided that they are used wisely – the dimensions can help designers to become sensitive to cultural variation.

Socio-cultural dimensions for designers - With the idea that products can mediate relationships that are formed by culture, I studied the barriers and opportunities for designers involving the use of these established dimensions. The level of abstraction required to approach cultural differences appeared to be helpful. It serves as a sort of tool to communicate about culture, and to structure cultural insights gleaned from, for example, field studies. However, the names of the dimensions are not always clear to designers, and are therefore misunderstood (such as the Masculinity dimension). Furthermore, cultural scores are not appropriate in design projects for several reasons *(van Boeijen, 2015)*. Firstly, they are based on average scores involving large populations. The people who filled in the survey form do not necessarily represent the specific generation or subculture for which you are designing. Secondly, your intended users might live in various countries. Most products are not used within one country only, and they are used across national borders. Thirdly, scores are by default based on measurements that were taken in the past, and they may not be currently relevant or useful for an envisaged future situation. As a result, scores are useful to sensitise with regard to *possible* value orientations but not to *predict* or to *prescribe* what to do. This means that you need to be very careful as regards the significance of these scores. They should not be dominating factors in your design direction. To overcome the barriers and make good use of the opportunities, an alternative set of dimensions that is aligned specifically with the work of designers, eas needed. *(van Boeijen, 2015)*

The American comedy series 'Seinfeld' liked to play with cultural framing and the resulting confusion. In 'The Wink,' Seinfeld inadvertently squirts grapefruit juice into George's eye over breakfast. This results in an irritation that causes an involuntary wink that makes all George's conversations awkward, as the tic is interpreted by some as having a significant meaning.

In what ways can we identify cultures?

'We recognise an involuntary tic and a conspiratorial gesture. Recognizing the action, its possible meanings, and discerning the intended meaning, is about understanding culture. We do this all the time — most of the time without noticing — trying to figure out what is really happening.'
(Stinson, 2018)

This section introduces distinctions, such as global culture, subculture, and folk culture. It looks at what we mean by these terms, and at how they are relevant for designers.

Cultural identity - In the first section, the concept of identity was approached from an individual perspective. You were invited to reflect on what identity could mean for yourself. In this section, we will elaborate on the identification of people as members of groups. Individual identity emphasises our *uniqueness:* the ways in which we differ from person to person; conversely, cultural identity highlights our *sameness:* the manner in which we differ from group to group as well as what we have in common within the group.

Before reading further, take a pen and a piece of paper, and draw an island. What kind of island did you draw? Now continue reading. Most people draw an island that looks like a circle surrounded by water and features one or two palm trees. The image does not reflect what most islands in the world actually look like, and yet we usually draw them that way, because it is how they are often depicted in the media, in advertisements, in films, and in other forms of visual communication. The stereotype image is rooted in our brains, and has come to constitute the identity of an island.

Cultural identity defined: sameness and uniqueness - For several reasons, the concept of cultural identity is a difficult one. As with the island exercise, you run the risk of stereotyping when trying to characterise cultures. General descriptions of a culture do not do justice to individual people or to subcultures within the specific culture.

Popular culture plays a major role in shaping the lens through which we view racial, sexual, and gender identity. Hip-hop and rap, genres created by poor black youngsters in the Bronx, have felt the impact of demonisation and stereotypes. Lil Nas X, the 20-year-old, gay, black, cowboy-hat-wearing rapping rock star is questioning and changing the way our society organises culture and the status quo around identity in his lighthearted video 'Old Town Road'.

Cultural identities are influenced by diverse factors such as religion, ancestry, skin colour, language, class, education, profession, skill, family, and political attitudes. Nation is a large factor in cultural complexity, as it constructs the foundation for an individual's identity but may contrast with one's cultural reality. Categorisations are always full of tensions and contradictions that can be destructive as well as creative and positive.

Consequently, people feel excluded and even offended. By the same token, we sometimes want to be identified as members of a certain group, because that gives a sense of belonging; it feels safe. First, let us take a closer look to be able to answer the question of what constitutes cultural identity. One possible answer is that cultural identities reflect common historical experiences and shared cultural codes, which provide us with *stable, unchanging and continuous frames of reference and meaning*. In the Netherlands, for example, there are certain products that have been used for decades, and that now serve – albeit in a superficial manner – as a reference to what is known Dutch culture. The cheese slicer, the Dutch bicycle, Delft blue pottery, and tulips are all objects that give meaning to the Dutch identity. The souvenir industry very happily makes use of these stable, unchanging symbols. They represent the Netherlands, and, as such, they contribute to the identification of a country. However, as with the island example, the stories behind the significance are not necessarily true. The above-mentioned products – or at least their concepts – did not originate in the Netherlands. A Norwegian, Thor Bjørklund, invented the cheese slicer in 1925; the Dutch bike originated in England; Delft blue pottery was initially copied from Chinese porcelain in the 17th century; and tulip bulbs were first imported from Turkey. The souvenir examples such as cheese slicers and tulips are superficial, of course, but the same process of cultural identification is happening in more subtle ways. What we nowadays know as Dutch Design, for instance, is identified as Dutch thanks to the designers who grouped together and developed a common story and to the media that disseminated it. Such stories about a culture's identity evolve into *myths*: namely, widely held but false beliefs or ideas that are passed on from generation to generation. Another possible answer regarding the question of cultural identity is that as well as the *many points of similarity, critical points of deep and significant difference* also constitute what our cultural identity is, or rather – because

A portmanteau is a linguistic blend of words. Lewis Carroll first used it in this sense in his book 'Through the Looking-Glass' (1871). Humpty Dumpty explains to Alice the practice of combining words: 'You see it's like a portmanteau – there are two meanings packed up into one word'. Britain's exit from the European Union became known as 'Brexit'. It can also be applied to objects. The spork is the do-it-all eating tool, combining spoon and fork, in this case with a bonus bottle/can opener.

The nature of the impact of the cultural arena changed with the advent of the Internet. It brought together groups with shared cultural interests who would previously have been more likely to integrate into their own real-world cultural arena. This plasticity allows people to feel a part of society wherever they go.

history has intervened – what our cultural identity has become. This second possibility is more dynamic. It recognises that cultural identities develop over time. This is a more dynamic view, and although the concept of cultural identity is problematic – designers should not ignore it. As long as there are people who want to be identified as a member of a certain group (large or small), they will use the designed world to meet that need. Designers could anticipate that need in ways that go beyond bland stereotypes, and/or help to deconstruct the ones that are undesired and, moreover, dangerous.

Cultural identity in design - Designers apply the uniqueness and sameness theory for the identification of brands and products. The Coca Cola bottle, for instance, was a great success due to its unique shape (inspired by the gourd-shaped cocoa bean, although the plant has nothing to do with the drink's ingredients); it was able to be recognised even if it were in pieces on the ground or being handled in the dark. Changes have been implemented over the years, but in such a way that the product's recognisability has not been affected.

Companies often make use of sameness deliberately so that customers are able to recognise (to identify) their brand over a long period of time. Cars are also given different shapes in such a way that they meet new requirements while at the same time sustaining their brand identity. You might wonder whether the need to stick to the same formal design language slows down developments. Insights into aerodynamics, for example, can provide us with a universal notion about the ideal shape for a car; however, the result would be cars that looked increasingly alike. Because brands require recognition, the shapes of cars change slowly. The on-going need for simultaneous distinction and recognition is ultimately not sustainable.

Because some new products are so unique that they cannot be classified in an existing category, new categories and names arise. This, for instance, is the case when two functions that were first fulfilled and identified in separate product categories come together in a new one. These blends, called portmanteau, include brunch (breakfast and lunch); burkini (bikini and burka); and emoticon (emotion and icon); and are also used for brand names such as Pinterest (pin and interest) and Microsoft (microcomputer + software).

Rembrandt is again examined for educational purposes and to look at the glorification of Dutch identity. It seems strange to revere artworks in which no Dutch people alive today had any part. People often have an interest in fleshing out the past with imaginary 'facts'. During World War II, art historian Julius Langbehn considered Rembrandt to be 'the most German of all German artists'.

In the 19th and the first half of the 20th century, Dutch artists and their works were described using catchwords having moral connotations, such as realistic, healthy, simple, homely, sincere, and honest. An artist like Jan van Goyen was a glorious champion of Dutch identity. In the beginning of the 20th century, terms like decadence, disease, and contamination were generally applied to everything that was considered to be 'alien'. [9]

Questioning a certain formal design language can also be liberating. When developing a medical product, for example, you might ask yourself whether it should fall into the medical category. Reconsidering the category can have a destigmatising effect; this also applies to products that are designed specifically for men or for women. You might ask yourself whether the categories are still up to date.

What are your boundaries? Earlier, we framed culture as comprising a group of people that share values and practices. We then looked at how people can be identified individually and as a group. But how do we set the boundaries? There are so many different ways to group people. It is possible to identify many groups, especially in highly economically developed areas where people move around. And in a virtual world, people are not even bound to a specific physical place. Cultural boundaries are not fixed and cannot be strictly defined. In fact, people belong to different groups, and these cultural groups can also change. Nevertheless, it is useful to specify and to define whichever group you are initially focusing on and at what level. You can look, for example, at culture on a national level, where boundaries are set by nationality – where people are raised or where they live right now. You can also consider region, social class, generation, religion, profession, gender, the political party people belong to, family, and so on. Being specific helps you to know where to dig deeper in order to understand certain practices, thereby gaining rich insights and discovering possible blind spots with regard to culture and contextual differences. The nature of your project will dictate how the boundaries are to be set; they just need to be relevant for your project. In the next section, you will be introduced to a few helpful distinctions.

Artist Roy Villevoye emphasises the subjectivity of the outsider's gaze and the often unintended effects of cultural coding. The work above, entitled 'The fifth man', was made in 2003 after traders from Indonesia started importing and selling Bin Laden T-shirts in the occupied territories of New Guinea. The way the Asmat people relate to mass produced T-shirts is quite different from what is customary in the West. Torn and tattered T-shirts are not a sign of poverty but a deliberate manipulation that adds ornamental value. The Asmats are unfamiliar with the cultural and political messages depicted.

A street in Hong Kong is called Rednaxela Terrace. Traditionally, Cantonese was written from top to bottom or right to left. Probably a city clerk that did not know English accidentally transcribed the correct name 'Alexander' in the wrong order.

Global and local cultures The term global culture refers to the globalisation phenomenon, and to how it has led to the fusion of cultures. Some aspects that once were peculiar to a specific culture can be found in local cultures where originally, they had nothing to do with those cultures' values and practices.

As a result, bridges have been constructed between cultures that previously had no or little relationship, thereby enriching the international cultural scene. Through this process of globalisation, cultures become more alike, sharing increasingly similar consumer products and ways of life. Owing to technology, such as the Internet and other developments that contribute to globalisation, national and local cultures are influenced by each other, resulting in similar kinds of consumer goods and economic interests. But be careful. Even if we all use the same products, their meaning can differ totally from culture to culture. In one culture, for example, a photocopy machine is a necessary device that takes up space, and, if possible, could be better replaced by a copying service. In another culture, however, the physical presence of this machine is important, because it depicts the economic status of the company. Moreover, over time these products are attuned to local needs.

Despite the positive effect of a shared understanding, global culture can also be considered as something negative in those instances where a stronger culture absorbs and transforms local people, thereby suppressing aspects of the original cultures, and throwing the baby out with the bathwater. From an economic perspective, companies might strive for the 'one-size-fits-all' solutions that serve large markets, but then

In Europe, St. Nicholas is the Catholic patron saint of children. This figure of generosity and benevolence, returns every year on December 5th to reward children who have been good. He is accompanied by menacing counterparts whose job is to punish children who have been bad. Parts of Germany and Austria dread the beastly Krampus who shows on the same night. A more modern take on the tradition involves drunken men dressed as devils chasing and beating people in the streets.

Cultural diversity is the quality of diverse or different cultures, as opposed to monoculture, or a homogenisation of cultures, akin to cultural decay. The world would be a dull place if everybody agreed on everything.

we might overlook the human need to feel a sense of belonging, to share a specific identity. We might also ignore the possibilities with regard to people who live at the base of the economic pyramid (4 billion out of a world population of 7.8 billion), who are bound to one place, and who are perhaps virtually but not physically connected to this global village. Furthermore, we might ignore cultural practices that were sustainable in the past – appropriate for the geographical situation and climate – and that due to globalisation are disappearing and being replaced by less sustainable solutions. Global norms and standards increasingly define our practices, and once they become established, it is difficult to get rid of them.

New Year's Eve: a global tradition? Every year, on the 31st of December, every hour of the full twenty-four, we can view on our TV sets or other devices dramatic and often awe-inspiring displays of fireworks from all over the world. This ritual – developed originally in China to scare away demons – has become an event that is celebrated globally. Although all displays make use of the same types of fireworks, many local rituals and meanings are incorporated. In Spain, for example, the fireworks ritual is accompanied by the eating of twelve grapes at the stroke of midnight, whereas the Irish apparently bang bread against the walls to beat off bad luck. Moreover, many cultures celebrate the start of a new year on different dates, such as the Lunar New Year in China; Nowruz in Iran, and Odunde in Nigeria, which is celebrated on the second Sunday in June. A design intern at a Dutch airline developed a calendar and

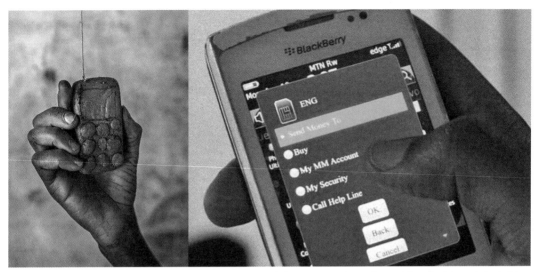

Displaced children building new lives in refugee camps create their own entertainment by moulding clay into archetypical toy tools. In many countries a mobile phone is a gateway to opportunities. In Africa it allows customers to deposit and withdraw money from a network of agents that includes airtime resellers and retail outlets acting as banking agents. The service has been lauded for providing millions of people in low-income countries with a formal financial system and reducing crime.

In 2017, more than 1.2 trillion photos were taken. This photo boom is related to the integration of digital cameras in smart phones and the rise of social media sites. This development has radically changed the way we look at the world around us and at ourselves. Freed from all restrictions of time and place, we have become non-stop exchangers of categorised words and images.

cards to be used by airline crews to remind them of specific festivities in order to celebrate them with passengers when appropriate. A first trial showed an increased rate of customer satisfaction. This illustrated how local and global practices could be brought together through design.

The mobile phone: a global design? Next to the T-shirt, jeans, and sneakers, the mobile phone is probably the most prototypical example of a global design. Ask a child in any place in the world to draw a phone, and he or she will likely draw a rectangular shape with one button. And who does not take selfies nowadays? However, when we delve more deeply into phone usage and its context, we perceive differences. One of the observations about the use of mobile phones in India was that many people shared their mobile phones with family members and friends *(Lindholm et al., 2003)*, although the mobile phone had been designed originally for individual use. This sharing has led to the notion of designing multiple address books to be used in one mobile phone, so that each user can refer to his or her personal contact list. In addition, the torch function appeared to be far more relevant in rural areas where the nights are really dark, and can be dangerous because of scorpions hiding in the shoes, people need for their walk to the toilet. M-Pesa is an example of another function that became enormously important in informal economies. The mobile phone-based money transfer platform supports people who cannot access formal banks. These examples illustrate that both local and global thinking in design do go together.

Designing for across the globe: three approaches - From an economical perspective, many companies will aim for a global approach to make sure they are able to max-imise the market and reap the most profit. The question arises as to how designers should act with regard to globalisation. Three approaches can be considered. One option is to start with a more basic design with characteristics that are based on a universal understanding of human behaviour. Marieke de Mooij states that new

In the Japanese movie 'Tampopo' (1985), an old monk explains to a young man how to eat ramen according to the Zen tradition. Yet ramen is the Japanese equivalent of fast food in our modern culture. Film director Juzo criticises the sometimes over-spiritualised Japanese traditions that lack any real meaning. The whole film is based on the notion that Japan is a mix of tradition and modernism, of spirituality and consumerism. Nevertheless, respecting animals is a fundamental Zen value.

The electric coffee pot from Gorenje, known as a Turkish coffee pot, makes reference to the traditional coffee maker. From an ergonomic perspective, the long handle ensuring that the person handling the pot did not burn his or her hand is no longer needed yet remained as a cultural signifier. The form of the base with the indicator light refers to the traditional fire.

products, such as the computer and the mobile phone, seem at first to be global designs that target a global market, and over time are tuned to the needs of specific cultures. The mobile phone, for example, was initially designed on a 'one-size-fits-all' basis, but specific local needs were discovered over time and were taken into account. *(Marieke de Mooij, 2004)* Another option is to start from the local situation and then later attune the design to a global market. The advantage of this approach is that the designer will dig deeper into people's specific context, which can lead to a richer understanding and more comprehensive ideas. In a later stage, when scaling up the market, the design will be evaluated and attuned to other cultural groups. An example is the Nespresso coffee machine, which is based on typical Italian coffee makers but has been adjusted to become a more easily used and more globally acceptable product. A third option is to work simultaneously in different cultural contexts, and to learn from the differences while designing, thereby finding common ground for a global version of the design.

National cultures: synthetic or true National cultures are defined by the set of norms, behaviours, beliefs, and customs that exist within the population of sovereign nations. International companies attune their management and other practices to the national cultures in which they operate.

Nations can be seen as historically constructed communities of people that not only share but also cherish certain norms, values, and practices, such as language, law, traffic rules, quality norms, money, national television, celebrations and festivals, food and drinks, music, rituals, flags, souvenirs, cars, and so forth. National borders define to which country or countries we belong. A popular name for national cultures is 'passport cultures'. This sense of belonging develops historically over time, and is maintained through the telling of stories, which are often myths; the stories told are not necessarily true, but they are important because they are the glue that bonds people together.

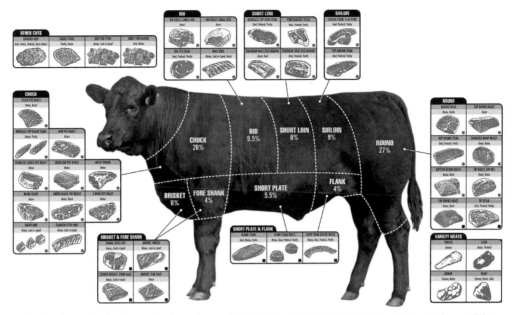

After hunting and gathering, most cultures have switched to agriculture and livestock farming. It has a long tradition of 'experimental' animal breeding, but today genetic traits of different organisms are mixed and matched. Industrial livestock farming is designed to maximise production and minimise costs. Unfortunately, it is also a major driver of global environmental degradation and loss of biodiversity.

Between 1820 and 1975, the agricultural production around the world doubled four times. In 1800 it was to feed a world population of one billion people and in 2020 of 7.8 billion. During this period, the number of workers involved in agriculture decreased dramatically. In 1940, every farm worker in the USA supplied an average of 11 consumers, while today every worker serves up to 90 consumers. About 70 billion farm animals are used annually to produce meat, dairy and eggs.

Within a country, especially large countries like China, India, Brazil, India, and Russia, but even in small countries, there are many subcultures that have their origins in ethnic similarities, religion, local dialects, and so on. People often feel that they have more in common within a subculture than the culture that is defined by national borders. Especially for those people who can move around freely, crossing national borders, the concept of a national identity might be meaningless. However, particularly to people who are tied to a specific place this concept of national identity might be very meaningful. Whatever the case, it is important to realise that in a globalising world the nation is a synthetically constructed concept that calls for a sensitive approach.

The nature of your project will determine how you use information and apply your knowledge about cultures on a national level. As stated in the section on socio-cultural dimensions for designers, you cannot use national scores measured along the cultural dimensions to predict human behaviour, but you can use them to sensitise for possible variation. You can also use them to explain certain findings from qualitative design research. Most important is to keep an open mind with regard to possible exceptions, and to the possibility of grouping people (if grouping is needed anyway) in many different ways, not only by nation.

Designing for national cultures: find the appropriate story - Because there are so many subcultures within a country, you might ask whether it makes sense for designers to approach cultures on a national level and to compare, for example, Chinese culture with Dutch culture. To a certain extent, it makes sense indeed, and is even necessary.

▶ *National regulations and norms:* First of all — as stated earlier — because of regulations, such as norms regarding the safety of toys, baby seats in cars, electrical wiring, and so on — national borders still matter. Before you start printing out a page, for instance, you set the default to Letter or A4, and some of you have probably checked bicycle parts

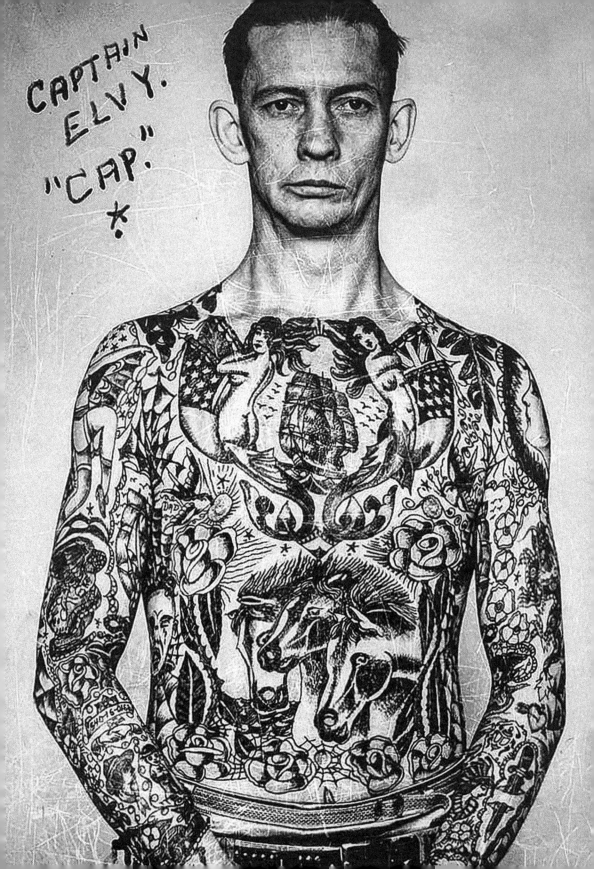

Individuals tend to think of themselves as projecting a certain physical appearance, a certain position of social entitlement, or lack thereof. The term 'residual self-image' was popularised in fiction by the 'Matrix' series, where persons who existed in a digitally created world would subconsciously maintain the physical appearance that they had become accustomed to projecting. [10]

for inches versus millimetres. In his book on the Norm=Form exhibition, Timo de Rijk illustrates by means of many examples how industrial standardisations increasingly determine the shape of products *(de Rijk, 2010)*. Companies even take national regulations and standardisations to be a competitive advantage through what is referred to as techno-regulation: technology with intentionally built-in mechanisms to influence people's behaviour *(Koops, 2008)*. Designers can of course simply take national regulations and norms into account in their designs, but perhaps they might also look for possibilities of combining or merging regulations and norms from different nations.

▶ *Stories and myths to be identified:* The distinction of national cultures makes sense when people explicitly want to be identified by their nation – think of games of sport, Olympics and Paralympics, and the European Song Festival – but also if they design for national institutes, such as the police or a government ministry. Organisations want to make use of national identities to 'tell stories that sell'. True and false stories about countries are told through design (e.g. statues of heroes, national hymns, clothing, national festivals, souvenirs, food, music, and many other expressions of our material world). By means of a historical analysis, you can find out and develop the story that fits your design best.

▶ *Preferred value orientations:* As previously mentioned, certain patterns of human behaviour are based on preferred values and can be explained by elements of the national culture. A comparative study on the credibility of websites, for example, showed that Spanish and German websites each need a different form if they are to be perceived as being credible. The study illustrated that text and figures add more to the credibility of German websites, while pictures of people improve the credibility of Spanish websites *(Snelders et al., 2011)*. The comparison elicits differences and, as a consequence, new possibilities for design. A comparison can also help to find the common ground if you want to design a website that fits all or several countries and is thereby attuned to local preferences. Is it appropriate to use a national flag to indicate a specific language or can we think of other ways?

Subcultures: dying or booming A subculture is a smaller culture comprised of a group of people within the main culture in a society; it differs from the main culture in some ways, but it also has many aspects in common.

People in a subculture can be from different social classes and ethnic minorities, but they can also be distinguished on the basis of their lifestyle or, for example, because they belong to the same sports club, profession, company, and so on. People of course can belong to different subcultures. When a student joins a rugby team, he enters a subculture with its own type of clothing, rules, and rituals, such as the loud singing of club songs and drinking beer after the match. The same student may also be member of a classical choir, which has totally different practices. Obviously, the music and dress codes were different, as were the ways in which most people in each group dealt with gender roles (i.e. separated for rugby and more equal in the choir). Nevertheless, somehow members of subcultures cherish certain common values as well, such as a strong sense of belonging to a group, maintained through language, rituals, behaviour, artefacts, and so on. Some people argue that in an increasingly globalised world,

Today, tattooed body decorations can be seen on the arms and ankles of self-declared rebels around the globe. Contemporary tattooing in the West can be traced to the 15th century, when European pilgrims would mark themselves with reminders of locations they had visited, as well as the names of their hometowns and spouses to help identify their bodies should they die during their travels. The attraction of tattoos for itinerant populations are obvious, since they cannot be lost or stolen, and they do not encumber an already heavily burdened traveller. It is no surprise that they were once inextricably associated with sailors and outcasts.

75

In the 18th and 19th century, a duel was an arranged engagement in combat between two people, with matched weapons, in accordance with agreed-upon rules. The tradition of duelling was originally reserved for male members of the nobility. However, in the 19th century it extended to those of the upper classes generally. After losing its distinctiveness for the nobility, adherents to the ritual gained 'satisfaction' – i.e. restored one's honour – by demonstrating a willingness to die for it. From 1921 until 1971, Uruguay was one of the few places where duels still took place and were fully legal.

The dual was once a widespread pheno-menon. In Manipur, India, duels were car-ried out according to a strictly defined code of ethics. Allowing the opponent to shoot an arrow first was considered particularly courageous. A warrior caste considered it shameful to die in bed, and often arranged a 'combat charity' if a warrior felt he had little time left to live. With a few attendants, he would challenge another king to a duel in order to arrange the time and manner of his own death, and to ensure he would die fighting.

subcultures are no longer relevant for designers. There are so many subcultures, and they are changing so quickly that they might become meaningless, especially for designers who aim for sustainable solutions. On the one hand, products designed for rapidly changing lifestyles and trends are not sustainable, and should not be leading in the design; on the other hand, there are subcultures – e.g. minorities – that could be empowered through design.

Designing for subcultures: sustainability considerations - Designers and companies are quite happy to take advantage of this human desire to belong to groups and to be identified by others as members of groups. They design and sell all kinds of useful – and unfortunately less useful and unsustainable – products that are geared to helping us communicate that we are members of the same 'tribe'. It depends on you and your project what to do: whether to design for an existing subculture, for a new subculture, or to avoid the notion of subculture and try to include as many as people as possible. There is one crucial question that designers always need to answer: 'Whom do I intend to include, and whom do I intend to exclude?' After all, designing for everybody is designing for nobody.

High, low, pop, and mass cultures: mind the stigma High culture refers to those manifestations of culture that express artistic and intellectual value. Low, Pop, and Mass cultures refer to cultural manifestations that are mostly produced for and sold to the majority of people.

Fine art (paintings, sculptures, video art), literature (novels, poems, essays), but also culinary arts (related to cooking and eating), clothing, and music are well-known

Jeff Koons borrowed the idea from Andy Warhol that, in a godless world saturated by media, art itself was just another commodity, albeit having extraordinary added value. In line with a western culture of free capitalism, Koons undertook an extensive study of what the contemporary artist needs to do to become rich. To achieve this, Koons carefully constructed a public image that depicted him as a scandalous character. Gift shops in museums ride the same wave, selling affordable mass-produced art items to the masses.

Since the Romantics, artists have been defined as rebels, and as prophets who allow the viewer to perceive a more profound and extensive reality. However, we have now embarked upon a new and harder-edged age. Some critics contend that contemporary art has largely become an asset used by wealthy buyers to borrow, trade on, and even defer capital gains taxes. The unprecedented availability of private wealth together with an equally large deficit of social and cultural capital might explain the inordinately high prices being paid for works from a small selection of celebrity artists.

categories of expressions of high culture. These categories are mostly known and appreciated by small groups in society, which are frequently seen by others as being elite, creating their own language and rules in order to wield power and enjoy certain privileges. The opposite of high culture is low culture. Actually, the terms low culture and high culture have a negative connotation, as if there is a certain inferiority or superiority, respectively, regarding people who are recognised as being members of either one of these groups. Alternative terms for low culture are mass and popular culture. They refer to cultural manifestations that are mostly produced for and sold to ordinary people. But who precisely are ordinary people? Because if you are genuinely curious about people, then every single person is unique, so what then does ordinary actually mean? At the very least, it refers a large number of people, the majority that buys and uses mass-produced, standardised – and often short-lived – products. In general, these kinds of products are not very expensive and are usually not of high quality when it comes to, for example, durability. But because of digitisation and new production techniques such as 3D printing, products that are designed intentionally for the masses can be adapted to appeal to individual preferences. For that reason, thanks to globalisation and technology, the boundaries between high and mass culture somehow appear to fade away. Or do they? On the contrary, together with the increasing difference between the very rich and the rest of the population, the manifestations of high and mass culture are maintained.

Between art and kitsch - Artists play with or criticise borders between high and mass culture. The contemporary artist Jeff Koons' sculpture 'Ushering in banality' is an enlarged version of a mass-produced object found in the south of Germany in the 19th century. By enlarging the size and downsizing the number into a single and very expensive piece, the artist is questioning the meaning of this manifestation of vernacular or folk culture, making fine art banal or the banal special, depending on how you want to look at it: something between art and kitsch.

Souvenirs in museum shops, with prints of famous works of art by painters such as Van Gogh and Monet on scarves, mugs, bags, T-shirts, and so on, are certainly kitsch to me. It is interesting though to see how close art and kitsch 'live together under one roof'.

Funeral rites pre-date modern Homo sapiens, and have existed since at least 300,000 years ago. Funeral customs are a highly predictable, stable force in communities, and tend to be characterised by five 'anchors': significant symbols, gathered community, ritual action, cultural heritage, and transition of the dead body. The roots of the Day of the Dead, celebrated in contemporary Mexico, go back some 3,000 years. Family members provided food, water, and tools to the deceased in order to help their souls on the difficult journey to Mictlán, the land of the dead. In the 16th century, Spanish conquistadors added traditions from All Saints Day and All Souls Day.

ashiko (literally 'little stabs') is a form of decorative stitching traditionally used to reinforce areas of wear or, using patches, to repair worn places or tears . The embroidery uses special sashiko thread and a specifically designed needle. Considered a beautiful surface embellishment, modern-day sashiko stitching is not restricted to the traditional indigo-coloured fabric.

Dying once was was a group experience, affecting every aspect of home life. The spectre of death materialised in the form of animals: we can find death in the form of a white goose, or a large black dog. Owls, active at a time when most are asleep, were considered a link between the world of the living and dead. The key ritual around funerals was a series of magical practices, which would relieve the dying of their agony, and the living of their fear. In many cultures it was important to bury the deceased with significant personal items for their journeys in the herafter, often including certain vices like cigarettes, alcohol or tobacco.

Designing for high and mass culture: a great source of inspiration - Artists are often sensitive to social developments, and can reflect critically because they distance themselves from commercial interests; they are therefore the antennas of society. Designers who are usually more influenced by commercial interests can use the work of artists as a moral compass and source of inspiration. The notion of differences can also be used to close the gap by redesigning things that initially are accessible to the 'happy few'. Affordable plastic trombones, for example, were used in an educational programme that aimed to bring classical music to children in disadvantaged areas. Sponsored by a foundation, children in primary school learned to listen to classical music and to play in an orchestra.

Folk cultures: the value of traditions Folk culture is often associated with local traditions, historical continuity, and a sense of place and belonging. Communities create expressions of culture that unify them in such a way that their identity is formed, recognised, and maintained over time. Folkloric manifestations seem to be sustained best around annual festivities and major life events such as birth, marriages, and death.

Stories from the past - Another example is Sashiko folk embroidery from Japan. With its origins in the Edo period in the 17th century, Sashiko embroidery was used initially to strengthen homespun clothing. Worn-out items were pieced together by means of simple running stitches in order to make new garments. This durable stitching increased the strength of the cloth. Later, Sashiko evolved into winter work in northern farming communities, when it was too cold to work outside *(Briscoe, 2005)*. The word Sashiko means little stabs, referring to the small stitches used in this form of needlework. The inspiration for traditional Sashiko designs is nature, and each pattern has its own special meaning. Sashiko-inspired designers looking for sustainable solutions have used this technique in their contemporary work.

Designing for folk cultures: folk cultures in design - Designing *for* folk culture seems to be a contradiction in terms, unless it is about renewing a certain ritual, for example, in a way whereby the tradition remains recognisable but also fits in with contemporary

After a trip to Korea in 1916, art critic and philosopher Yanagi Sōetsu (1889 -1961) founded the Japanese folk art movement 'mingei'. Mingei stands for folk craft, and emphasises the beauty of handmade everyday objects, such as ceramic dishes, textiles, teapots, and furniture. The makers were usually anonymous.

In the late 19th century, a design and social reform movement – named Arts and Crafts – originated in Europe. Its proponents are motivated by the ideals of its founders, William Morris and John Ruskin, who proposed that in pre-industrial societies, such as in the European Middle Ages, people achieved fulfilment through the creative process involving handicrafts. This was held up in contrast to what was perceived to be the alienating effects of industrial labour.

customs. But how might we use folk culture in design? You might wonder whether folk culture is interesting for contemporary consumers, since manifestations of folk culture are often perceived as old fashioned, and understood and appreciated only by small groups of people.

However, we can learn a great deal about a culture through its folkloristic traditions. They can tell us something about the history of a culture and about what is important to people in their local and everyday environments. In addition, as we saw in the examples, designers can view expressions of folk culture as a tremendous source of inspiration for new designs, not only for the sake of creating something new but also to contribute to people's desire to have a cultural identity. In fact, folk culture has always informed pop culture and even high culture. We must be careful, however, because a culture-related design mistake is easily made, and small mistakes can have significant consequences. Products can be designed to appeal to the majority of consumers, but the members of a specific culture can perceive a superficial use of symbols that are originally from their folkloristic ritual as being highly offensive.

Between cultural groups

Research shows that cultural diversity in teams stimulates creativity. But the encounter between multiple cultural groups can also lead to conflicts. In this section, a number of key concepts are explained and illustrated, with examples of what that can mean for design.

Dominant cultures versus minority cultures - In any society, a dominant culture is its main one, in which the majority of people share similar values and practices. These values and practices are often unconsciously taken for granted, and are considered to be what people refer to as 'normal'.

An advantage of a dominant culture is that shared values and practices function as a social glue that binds together different groups or classes, even regardless of their separate and distinctive interests. A disadvantage, however, is that people who do not know or want to share these values and practices may feel excluded. The dominant culture can become a problem if a critical reflection of these values and practices is

Totalitarian ideologies reduce society, with all its diversity and complexity of human experience, to a blunt dichotomy: light and darkness, good and evil, right and wrong, radical and reactionary. The Cultural Revolution in China under Mao provides a chilling example of the dangers of an excess of political homogeneity. In the years prior to the Cultural Revolution, the Party had cultivated an environment of extreme conformity by means of Maoist thought-reform campaigns. Nietzsche warned that 'the surest way to corrupt a youth is to instruct him to hold in higher esteem those who think alike than those who think differently'.

'There is no middle way!' became a popular slogan expressing the purity of mind that defined the communist Red Guards. Animated by the forces of purity and paranoia, these young idealists were well suited to the project of eradicating what was called 'the Four Olds': old customs, old culture, old habits, and old ideas. The Red Guards imposed a new symbolic order on an old world, without the clutter or caution based on life experience that could yield only mayhem.

missing, and if there is no acceptance of possible differences let alone a new common ground. We can identify dominant cultures only if there are minority cultures or subcultures as well. In design education and master's degree programmes, the group of students who also did their bachelor's degree at the same institution form a dominant culture that comes with a certain way of designing: namely, the terminology used, models and methods, and ideas about what comprises good design. The term 'concept', for example, typically means something different from one design culture to another. Students from other schools of design form the minority that is accustomed to different practices. A culture-sensitive design educator will be aware of the different groups, and will actively help to find common ground where necessary.

To be in the right or to be proved right - In the process of globalisation, minorities often need to adopt the practices of the more dominant cultures. Many practices from the United States of America and West-European countries, for example, have been widely adopted, such as the wearing of T-shirts, sneakers, jeans, and ties. Colour codes like pink for girls and blue for boys have also been spread all over the world. However, it was only in the second half of the 20th century that this gender division was colour coded, mainly for economical reasons. Companies started to make products specifically for women and men in order to sell more products and to make the different product categories more easily identifiable.

In 1876, Alexander Graham Bell was the first to be granted a United States of America patent for a device that produced a clearly intelligible replication of the human voice. Initially, phones were large machines leased in pairs to a subscriber, who had to arrange for a telegraph contractor to construct a line between them; now we have the mobile smartphone with its wireless connection to a global social network. They have become a digital extension of oneself.

When the first Spanish explorers first arrived in the Southern area (known today as the Yucatán Peninsula), they asked the natives what their country was named. The natives kept responding with a phrase that sounded like 'Yucatan', which in the native language meant 'I don't understand you'.

Designing in a dominant culture with minorities - The distinction 'dominant culture' can help you to rethink designs. With the example of pink for girls versus blue for boys, it is useful to know that it is a convention developed over the years and spread through the practices of the dominant culture. Designers could, for example, rethink colour code conventions; find out whether there were underlying principles of human behaviour that justified the colour coding; and find arguments for using the most appropriate colour. The distinction can also help you to be sensitive to minority cultures or subcultures that might be excluded from using your design. Finally, we can use design to bring people together.

Stereotypes and archetypes A stereotype is often a conventional and oversimplified conception, opinion, or image, based on the assumption that attributes exist that members of the group hold in common. Products often affirm these stereotypes. An archetype can be defined as a basic model of a product, representing the main characteristics of a class of products.

Pros and cons of designs for categorisation - The term 'stereotype' is generally used in categorising people, and it has a negative connotation; the term 'archetype' in the context of design is generally used for products, and it has a neutral connotation. Marketing often uses stereotypes of groups of people and related products because they are easy to recognise. And indeed, there is also a useful reason for it. This categorisation of people and things help us to organise our minds and to establish some order in a multi-formed and multi-coloured world. Unfortunately, however, stereotypes often do no justice to differences between people; moreover, if you hang on to these stereotypes, they will impede your creativity enormously. A pink electric shaver, for example, is a simplified notion of what women like: namely, just '*pink it and shrink it*' and you are done. The reality is much more complex, with the result that stereotypes are by default leaving out the nuances. People are represented as they are in stock photos that have been made expressly for marketing purposes.

Souvenirs created to market countries and cities are perhaps the most pronounced examples of stereotyping by design.

'Archetype' is used for artefacts, and is more neutral than the term 'stereotype'. In another discipline, the term 'prototype' is used, which is confusing because in design the term is used for three-dimensional modelling to simulate and evaluate product properties. A current example of an archetypical representation of the phones category is the one with just a rectangular surface and one circle. It depends both on our cultural background and our generation as to whether a product form can be recognised as the archetype for a specific product category. If you were to ask a 90-year-old and 20-year-old to draw a telephone', you could end up with two quite different representations. As with stereotypes, you might question whether you want to keep your design close to what people already know and are able to identify or to create something new that has the potential to become the new archetype.

Designing with the notion of stereotypes and archetypes - How can a designer avoid unwanted and stigmatising categorisations, since categorisation is also a way to create order in chaos? He or she may need some structure or a system in order to understand our world and to feel comfortable and safe. One strategy is through education, whereby designers learn to refine categories; to be more precise and nuanced; to learn true stories; and to break myths. Design can help to tell stories and to introduce new ones. Another strategy involves looking for abstract forms. It seems that designers in a globalising world try to avoid the risk of stereotyped cultural identification by making apps and other forms of communication abstract, thereby avoiding details that could be specific to a culture. With such designs, however, it seems that they also lose meaning and remain superficial. It is difficult to know what to do, but at least being sensitive to the possibilities can help designers to find a meaningful direction.

Value conflicts We experience inter-cultural conflicts when we find ourselves pulled in multiple directions as we try to respond to the various societal norms and role expectations we hold and care about.

Each of us has personal goals and values that direct our behaviour and daily practices. Although we are not always consciously aware of them, these goals and values may be 'awakened' by circumstances in a specific context. For example, with its layout and the presence of colleagues, our office environment may trigger work-related goals and values, such as productivity or professional accomplishment. Moreover, a specific context may trigger conflicting goals and values. For instance, working with a colleague who is also a close friend may spark a conflict between the value of benevolence (i.e. I value my friendship, and therefore want to avoid confrontation) and that of accomplishment (i.e. I value professional success, and therefore want to finish this project as effectively as possible). Such conflicts may at first seem undesirable, but in fact they can be transformed into highly valuable design opportunities.

Three types of conflict to take into account - Deger Ozkaramanli researches dilemma-driven design, which she defines as an approach that considers the emotional dilemmas of end-users as fruitful starting points for human-centred design activities *(Ozkaramanli, 2017)*. She defines dilemmas as 'the experience of being faced with two mutually exclusive choices, both of which touch upon personal concerns, and the simultaneous fulfilment of which is challenging if not impossible'. In a dilemma

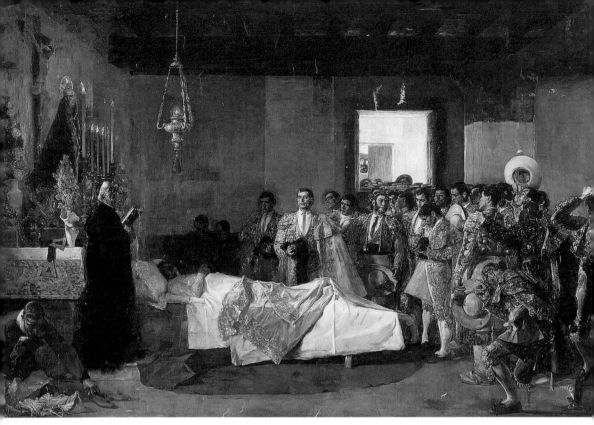

Bullfighting is a celebrated tradition in some countries but is illegal in most. It is controversial owing to animal welfare concerns, funding, and religion. Several forms of bullfighting exist where the bull is not physically harmed, drawing blood is rare, and the bull is allowed to return to his pen at the end of the performance. Spanish-style bullfighting is normally fatal for the bull, and can be fatal for the matador as well.

The bullfight is regarded as a demonstration of style, technique, and courage by its participants and as a demonstration of cruelty and cowardice by its critics. While there is usually no doubt about the outcome, the bull is not viewed by bullfighting supporters as a sacrificial victim but as a worthy adversary, deserving of respect in its own right.

situation, people experience mixed emotions with regard to each choice *(Ozkaramanli et al., 2016)*. Dilemma-driven design works particularly well in the beginning phases of the process (i.e. the fuzzy front end). This is when the challenge is being framed through exploring potential dilemmas relevant to the design brief, and through conceiving the first ideas on what to design in order to address the core challenge in the brief.

Deger linked dilemma-driven design to culture-sensitive design. Arguing that value conflicts are inspiring starting points, she distinguished between three potential value-related conflicts around which designers can formulate and design. These conflicts are based on Schwartz' taxonomy, in which value domains that sit opposite each other are the most likely to conflict, while those adjacent to each other have commonalities. Achievement versus benevolence, for example, is more likely to result in conflict than is benevolence versus universalism, where the values are situated next to each other *(Schwartz, 2006)*.

▸ *Intra-individual (internal) value conflicts:* As individuals, we hold many values, and in certain situations they come into conflict with each other. These internal conflicts are experienced in everyday life as dilemmas. The above-mentioned triggers – 'I value my friendship, and therefore want to avoid confrontation' versus 'I value professional success, and therefore want to finish this project as effectively as possible' – constitute an example of an internal value conflict experienced when professional and personal roles overlap.

▸ *Value conflicts between the individual and the cultural group:* We are all part of a larger national culture as well as smaller subcultures such as 'work' culture, 'student' culture, and so forth. On the one hand, we find it important to develop and maintain a feeling of belonging to these cultures. On the other hand, we may not always agree with or fully internalise all the values associated with that cultural group. For example, Eastern cultures value being humble about accomplishments *(Hao, 2019)*. In contrast, most Western work environments value and reward talking explicitly about achievements in the workplace. Here, the desire to belong to a culture (e.g. feeling connected and appreciated at work) is in conflict with individual value orientations (e.g. being humble about achievements).

▸ *Inter-group (intercultural) value conflicts:* As we zoom away from individual experiences, we observe different value orientations between diverse cultural groups, which lead to intercultural conflicts. Imagine a barbecue situation where meat eaters and vegetarians (two subcultures) talk about the social and ethical implications of eating meat. Such conversations often result in a conflict of the values held by each group. A similar yet more concerning situation is when the dominant cultural norms and expectations in a society are incompatible with those of minority groups living in the same society.

Designing for value-related conflicts - Deger argues that there are at least two main approaches to addressing value-related conflicts: 1) resolution through design, and 2) using design to raise awareness about the conflict in order to foster cultural sensitivity.

When dealing with people from other cultures, we have to pay careful attention to the failures of the human brain, which functions like a prediction machine. The main thing that gets in the way of clear communication is that people may not give one another an opportunity to create an expectation of failure.

▸ *Resolving the value-related conflict:* Design can simultaneously handle conflicting values in order to relieve cultural tensions. Deger gives an example from a large-scale innovation project in which she was involved *(Ozkaramanli et al., 2013)*. In this project, the dilemmas experienced during an afternoon tea ritual were taken as a starting point to develop new teatime snack concepts for a specific target group. The most remarkable cultural insight gained was that the food and the way it was served symbolised the host's love and care with regard to her guests. Some dilemmas were embedded in deeply held personal and cultural values. For example, the research team observed a significant tension between the host's wish to follow new trends and developments and the security of maintaining traditional practices. In the context of the project, this tension became apparent in the following dilemma. The host wanted to prepare new dishes for the occasion, but she feared that the guests would be more appreciative of traditional and familiar recipes. The project team tackled this predicament by offering packaged food products that combined new, unexpected forms and flavours with traditional ones as well as designing a brand identity that blended modern forms, colours, and patterns with traditional ones *(Ozkaramanli et al., 2013)*. Another example is from design students who created coasters that bore recipes for both meat and vegetarian burgers that can be used for a barbecue occasion. This intervention was helpful in two ways: first, to make sure that everyone had something to eat, and second, to moderate discussions that may have arisen by focusing on different aspects of being a meat eater or a vegetarian. In this way, the students aimed to resolve the conflict and to create an opportunity — by way of the coasters — to have a discussion around the topic.

▸ *Raise awareness about the value conflict:* It may not always be possible (or desirable) to design explicitly to resolve value conflicts, as resolving eliminates the cultural tension that can instead be used to raise awareness about the multiplicity of cultures and

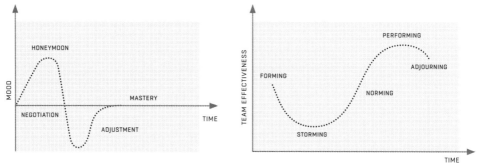

Similar to the culture shock model, Tuckman (1965) developed a model for team dynamics that follows five stages: Forming: Team members get to know each other; Storming: Some members will push against other's boundaries. Norming: Team members start to resolve issues on the basis of team dynamics. Performing: Once common ground has been established, the team can work on achieving its goals; Adjourning: The occasion on which team members split up after they have reached their goal.

During the 1990s, NASA launched a mission to mars called the Martian Climate Orbiter. The Orbiter would deploy a Martian Polar Lander on the surface of the planet for scientific measurements. The Orbiter and the Lander would then communicate with each other, and send any information back to Earth. Unfortunately, the Orbiter team used metric measurements, while imperial had been used on the Lander. This caused measurement problems from the very start of the months-long space voyage. When it came time to land the probe, NASA lost contact with the MCO, which either crashed on the planet or became lost somewhere in the universe.

viewpoints. The 'raising of awareness' strategy, therefore, is based on the premise that all cultures deserve attention, and that there is more than one 'valid' point of view. For example, in a project for the design of a food kit (a box with ingredients, tools, and a recipe to be sold in a supermarket), the designer wanted to raise awareness regarding two value orientations: 'openness to change versus tradition'. Her solution was to raise awareness by offering two recipes (in this case, pastel de nata [Portuguese custard tart]), showing that the user could choose and that both ways were equally acceptable.

Culture shock and acculturation Culture shock is the personal disorientation people feel when experiencing an unfamiliar way of life: for example, when visiting or migrating to a new country, or when moving between social environments. Acculturation is the process of cultural and psychological change that results from an interaction between cultures. A culture shock can be part of this process.

Phases and strategies - Culture shock is described in *four distinct phases*. The first phase is *Honeymoon*, in which everything is new, exciting, and interesting. This is the moment to identify what is different from one's own experience. It is the moment that we take photographs, write home, and describe everything that is new to us. The second phase is *Negotiation*, in which differences become apparent, problematic, and frustrating. This is the moment to reflect on our own and other people's values, norms, and practices, and on where they come into conflict. The third phase is *Adjustment,* in which strategies and new routines are developed to deal with the new situation. Some new practices will be easy to adopt while others will be more difficult to accept. The last phase is *Mastery*. This is the moment at which we deal successfully with both cultures; with the values and practices that are important and that are developed in the culture of origin; and with the values and practices that are typical for the other culture.

Acculturation: is a necessary process when people migrate from one culture to another, and the effects of acculturation can be seen at multiple levels in both interacting cultures. John Berry distinguishes *four strategies* for acculturation between ethno cultural groups *(Berry 2007)*: integration, assimilation, separation, and marginalisation. *Integration* is considered the most successful means of acculturation, in which both cultural groups (the dominant and the new one) will maintain their own cultural

When the Jewish Ghetto (from the Venetian word 'getto', 'to melt' in Italian) was built on the site of an old metal foundry in 1516, Venice was a major centre of commerce, noted for its cosmopolitan atmosphere and cultural diversity. But it was also a time when Venice was distrustful of anyone they considered to be outsiders. By confining Jews to a small island demarcated by two gates that were to be opened in the morning and closed at midnight, Venice simultaneously included and excluded that population. Outside the Ghetto, Jews had to wear certain distinguishing symbols – typically a yellow hat, scarf, or badge.

Despite al the restrictions, the crowded living conditions, and the intrusive surveillance, Venice's Jews managed to make the Ghetto a place where many types of traditions flourished. As a cosmopolitan crossroads with various languages, customs, cultures, and religious rites, the Ghetto was a city within a city, rich in diversity.

background but will also find new common ground where they share values and practices. This is similar to what is described regarding culture shock in the mastery phase. *Assimilation* is a process in which the ethnic group adjusts to the dominant culture but without maintaining much of its original culture. This might be comfortable for the dominant culture, but is not ideal for newcomers, especially for adults, because giving up deeply embedded values is difficult and painful. Another possibility is *Separation*, in which newcomers remain in their own cultural 'bubble' and do not adopt new values and practices. This is often difficult for the dominant culture to accept, and it is especially difficult for the younger generation of newcomers, as they need to switch between two cultural groups: that of their family culture and that of their school. Studies illustrate that in such situations young people may have difficulty in developing their identity. *Marginalisation* is the last and least healthy strategy. Here, people from a minority culture are confused and remain between worlds, so to speak. They neither adopt elements of the new culture nor do they maintain the culture in which they were raised. They are left in confusion, losing their sense of belonging and identity.

In a similar model, but on a societal level, Berry distinguishes the above four strategies in terms of multiculturalism, melting pot, segregation, and exclusion.

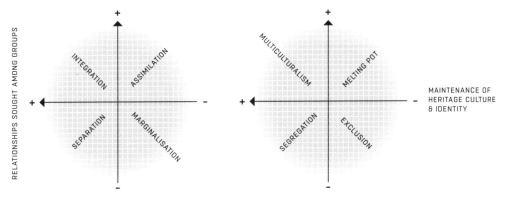

RELATIONSHIPS SOUGHT AMONG GROUPS

INTEGRATION   ASSIMILATION

SEPARATION   MARGINALISATION

MULTICULTURALISM   MELTING POT

SEGREGATION   EXCLUSION

MAINTENANCE OF HERITAGE CULTURE & IDENTITY

Four strategies in an acculturation process, based upon two issues: in ethno-cultural groups (left) and on a larger societal level (right) (Berry, 2005).

In the 1970s, a professor by the name John F.C. Turner, teaching in a new masters programme at MIT called 'Urban Settlement Design In Developing Countries', developed an idea surrounding the concept that people can build houses for themselves. Turner made the case that housing ought not be a static unit that is packaged and handed over to people. Rather, housing should be conceived of as an ongoing project in which residents are co-creators. Housing as a verb.

Design for integration - The stages of culture shock can be used to prepare for a local study and to become sensitive as regards deep and hidden values and norms. A pitfall of being in the honeymoon phase as an outsider is that everything that is new seems to be 'something of the other culture'. Not everything that is new is necessarily typical for the culture under examination. What is experienced as new can be a global practice that the outsider simply did not know yet, because he or she is unfamiliar with it. The observation can even also be an out-dated exception. Nevertheless, as an outsider, you can make considerable use of the moment at which you become sensitive to differences; for instance, you can identify practices that local people cannot easily articulate because they are not aware there are differences. Observations from an outsider can also help local people to reflect on their own culture.

When working on a topic that is completely new to you, it is useful to first study it in one's own culture. Once you are an expert, you are able to compare with other situations and see what might and might not be attuned to the new cultural context. The culture shock stages also help us to remember that there will be a moment at which it is necessary to take a stance. The negotiation stage triggers the question of to what extent does one follow the dominant values and practices of the targeted context.

Finally, with a little imagination, we, as designers, can also apply the four stages of culture shock to the manner in which new products – rather than cultures – can be experienced; first there is the honeymoon phase, in which enthusiasm about the newness dominates, but then comes a moment when we wonder whether we want to integrate the product or new technology into our lives.

In closing - In this section, we took a closer look into the concept of culture, sharpening our lens to look at culture in a way that is useful for designers. Various distinctions used in other disciplines such as anthropology and sociology were explained and illustrated with examples that resonate with the work of designers. Section 3 provides an overview of models and methods to be used to examine culture while designing; to design in a culture-sensitive way; and to evaluate designs from a culture-sensitive perspective.

Building half a house might just be the best way to make a community whole. Architect Alejandro Aravena and his firm Elemental pioneered the DIY approach in Chile. They designed half-built houses, called 'half a house', for low-income families. Over time, residents could turn the component parts of their basic sites into complete housing, and according to their own wishes. They would donate their labour and pay the cost of materials to finish the house. In the end, they owned what they had built.

MODELS AND METHODS

DESIGNING
WITH
CULTURE

This section introduces you to certain models and methods that can be used to examine and to design for culture. While applying them, you will become increasingly familiar with their possibilities. A method is simply a means and not a goal in itself. Therefore, select and fine-tune the methods according to your own preferences and projects; see also the introduction section in the Delft Design Guide, and its overview of perspectives, approaches, models, and methods for designing. (van Boeijen et al. 2020, 2nd ed.)

Historically, the prevailing notions of what was deemed sexually ethical have been tied to religious values. Many of the sexual practices in the world today, such as the custom and art of kissing, emerged in India, proliferating with early forms of globalisation. One factor in the change of values pertaining to sexual activities in the 20th century was the invention of new, efficient technologies for birthcontrol. The top image portraits Queen Victoria, Prince Albert, and their children in the early 19th century as an idealised family. Below the 'Dream of the Fisherman's Wife' by Katsushika Hokusai from the same era (1814).

LET'S GET STARTED

Now that you have a lens with which to examine culture, as well as examples in mind about what design can do, it is time to put culture sensitivity into practice. Although many models and methods exist with regard to understanding people within their context, few are developed specifically to look at people through a culture-sensitive lens.

To understand people requires knowledge of their cultural and moral values. The term 'Victorian morality', for example, can describe any set of values that espouse sexual restraint, low tolerance of crime, and a strict social code of conduct. During the Edo period in Japan (1603-1868), many ukiyo-e shunga artworks revolved around women and sea creatures, since any depictions of sexual activity between a man and a woman were seized. For the Samurai, shunga was a lucky charm to avoid death, while merchants believed them to be a protection against fires that could ruin their homes and businesses.

You might argue that this is not needed, because it is enough to examine people as part of a comprehensive whole. However, designers tend to understand people from a general perspective, using universal principles to explain their behaviour or focusing on individual needs and dreams. In contrast, the models and methods are constructed to help designers view people from a cultural perspective. And – as mentioned earlier – this does not mean that one perspective is enough. Ultimately, you need various lenses.

Models and methods are suggested in order to help you get started in applying culture- sensitive design. Some have been developed especially for purposes related to culture sensitivity, whereas others are variations on widely used design research models and methods. Underlying perspectives differ, however; for instance, are you looking as an *outsider*, comparing different cultural groups, or as an *insider* from within a culture? In each case, it is important to decide whether and in what way the models and methods are relevant to your project.

Why models and methods? In general, designers use models and methods to deal with the complexity of the act of designing. Models and methods can play different roles for you and your projects, like realising a design goal, organising the work that needs to be done and justifying and accounting for the work to stakeholders *(van Boeijen et al. 2020, 2nd ed.)*. The intention of the proposed models and methods in this book is to help you to:
- *focus your cultural lens;* knowing how and where to look at culture;
- *study culture;* building an understanding of the cultural context for which you design;
- *set a design goal;* making your intention towards the existing culture explicit;
- *generate ideas;* creating new ideas and concepts;
- *evaluate ideas and concepts;* checking the acceptability of your design.

Some definitions are given to ensure that we are on the same page in terms of what is meant by the various terms. They are ordered here from abstract to concrete:

▶ *Perspectives:* A perspective refers to the reason for the design activity. Perspectives are *descriptive* in nature; a perspective focuses on specific intended effects and qualities to strive for when doing design; for example, this could be the intention to create a bridge between two or more cultural groups through design.

▶ *Models:* In this context, a model is a representation of a theory about how to understand reality. Models are *descriptive* in nature; they describe how design happens; for example, the Circuit of Culture describes five meaning-giving processes that are used to understand culture.

▶ *Methods:* the regular and systematic ways or means of accomplishing something. Methods are *prescriptive* in nature; they describe ways of going about a design activity. A method offers a specific process for a design activity, and is used predominantly within a specific phase of design.

▶ *Tools:* the practical means that help designers to execute the activities described by the methods; for example, the Cultura canvas is a tool that comes with the method that describes how to use it.

▶ *Techniques:* the skills and abilities to use the tools and apply the methods.

The models and methods presented in this book have been developed in a specific design culture; therefore, they are representative of that culture and are influenced by its specific norms and values. In this design school, the development and education inherent in the methods are highly valued. This means that other ways of understanding culture-sensitive design can be valuable and effective as well. The lens proposed in this book is simply one way to approach culture in design.

'In contrast to what many people think, methods are not there to get to a solution more quickly but to slow you down, to avoid jumping to conclusions'. (Kees Dorst, 2018)

Emic and etic: your perspective - These terms refer to the perspective that you adopt to study culture. You need to be aware that you can examine culture from the perspective of an outsider as well as an insider. The *emic* approach refers to investigating a culture within the social group, which is from the perspective of the subject as an insider. The *etic* approach refers to examining a culture from the outside, which is from the perspective of the observer as a scientist, as an outsider. John Berry suggests that we should combine both perspectives in order to arrive at a complete understanding of a culture. Organisational studies on culture, measuring dimensions, are typically approaches from an etic (outsider) point of view: namely, through the outsider's comparison of cultures, an understanding of what is culture specific is developed. Ethnographic research is typically a cultural study from an emic (insider) point of view. Possible differences are not important; more important is to describe the present culture in all its manifestations. It is useful to know these two perspectives tot consciously choose your own and be able to align your view in discussion with others.

Outsider or insider: influence of your role The designer – as an outsider – needs to be aware of his or her influence on intended users. The intended users are the insiders who are members of one or more cultural groups. And it is not only the outsiders who are biased. Also insiders' reactions to outsiders have an impact on how one understands a culture.

In a study in Kenya, designers (outsiders) stated that – to their surprise – according to their Kenyan stakeholders, they had arrived late for an appointment. The Kenyans emphasised that the design team had promised to visit them within two weeks, but had failed to do so. The team had not expected the Kenyans to be strict regarding an appointment, as team members had experienced that people in the African culture were not as strict in their sense of time as those in the – in this case – European culture. The design team had not been able to see things from the perspective of the Kenyans (insiders), and therefore did not realise that their sense of the present would be valued differently; as a result, this provoked an interaction other than expected on the basis of culture-related information.

Culture-sensitive design methods can provide examples of dedicated means and strategies to avoid such biases. Moreover, methods can stress the importance of local research carried out by the designers.

Storytelling: collecting 'thick data' A way to understand a specific culture is through the stories that people share about their lives, their past, and their current practices. Designers use all kinds of creative methods and related tools to encourage people to talk, often focused on their individual stories and experiences. This section shows methods and tools designed to build an empathetic understanding of people with a focus on their experiences as part of one or more cultural groups. 'Healthy interpersonal relationships are

Anthropologist and outsider Lévi-Strauss (1908-2009) believed that the human mind thinks fundamentally in binary oppositions and their unification (the thesis, antithesis, synthesis triad), and that these are what make meaning possible. Furthermore, he considered the job of myth to be a sleight of hand, an association of an irreconcilable binary opposition with a reconcilable binary opposition, creating the illusion, or belief, that the former had been resolved.

'Objects are what matter. Only they carry the evidence that throughout the centuries something really happened among human beings.' (Levi Strauss)

the key to success. Facilitating appropriate social interactions among the participants and between them and the researcher may determine the success of the user session and the richness of the user stories' *(Chen Hao, 2019).*

Attune your methods Most design methods are developed in a Western European and North American design culture, and are also applied in these related user contexts. Research shows that these methods — most of them participatory — do not always work as intended in contexts unfamiliar to the designer, such as in projects for people who belong to the group that is seen as being at the base of the economic pyramid (BoP) or to the emerging markets, often in rural areas. They frequently live in non-Western cultures. In order to make full use of the involved participants', and taking into account both their weaknesses and strengths regarding the aim of these methods, it is important to attune the methods and their related tools and sessions to the specific context.

In participatory sessions such as Contextmapping, where participants are encouraged to express themselves freely, you need to adjust your methods to the local context. Participants need to feel safe and therefore must trust each other. They also need to be convinced that their time is not being wasted and that your project is credible. In certain subcultures, the creative tools that often come with these methods are perceived as childish, and therefore they do not contribute to the perceived credibility of your work.

In international projects, and particularly in BoP, language and differences in educational backgrounds are often challenging barriers. Differences in cultural values can sometimes lead to biases that can be avoided with good preparation and an open attitude towards unexpected and new situations. Most designers consider sensitising tasks to be made for their intended users, and not for themselves, but it is worth taking time to recall your own experiences and see the value in doing so' *(Chen Hao, 2019).*

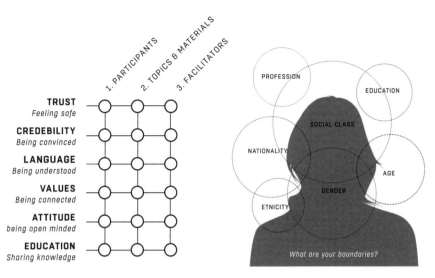

TRUST
Feeling safe

CREDEBILITY
Being convinced

LANGUAGE
Being understood

VALUES
Being connected

ATTITUDE
being open minded

EDUCATION
Sharing knowledge

1. PARTICIPANTS
2. TOPICS & MATERIALS
3. FACILITATORS

PROFESSION
EDUCATION
SOCIAL CLASS
NATIONALITY
AGE
GENDER
ETNICITY

What are your boundaries?

Use this checklist for the preparation of participatory sessions. Three main aspects of participatory sessions should be considered: 1. Selection of participants. Regarding differences and commonalities within the group; 2. Selection of topics, form, and content of materials, structure of the sessions, and location. Regarding the sensitivity of the topic, and the meaning that the topic and materials evoke; and 3. Selection of the role and attitude of the facilitator(s). Regarding gender, style, and number of facilitators.

Language and communication Innumerable books and other resources are available on the topic of cross-cultural communication. This book only highlights specific aspects that could be useful in the context of design projects.

Erin Meyer explains how communication styles can differ and lead to misunderstanding (*'Listen to the air of Culture Map', 2014*). People in high-context cultures are accustomed to 'listen to the air', which means that messages are implicit, depending on the situation and relying heavily on non-verbal language. This is in contrast to low-context cultures, in which information is communicated in a direct, explicit, and precise manner. Design students from all over the world that come to study in the Netherlands confirm that they needed to get used to the very direct communication style of Dutch people. At first, they found it embarrassing, but later they appreciated the straightforwardness of this type of communication. For people who are used to a very direct communication style, the pitfall is that they often think their directness conveys trust: namely, 'If you do not say it straight, you are not trustworthy'. However, in contextual research — and the situation is similar in international business — you cannot expect there to be enough time to learn each other's ways of communication; therefore, you need to be sensitive to possible differences, and to adapt where possible in order to be understood as intended.

A frequent barrier encountered in international design projects is that facilitators often do not share a common language. They do not speak the local language, and therefore have difficulties communicating, especially with non-formal participants. In translations done by interpreters, information often gets lost; long conversations are translated into just a few sentences in which only the facts are summarised, and no emotions or feelings on the part of the interviewees are conveyed. The answers are adjusted and interpreted according to the social situation (socially acceptable answers with biases). In cross-cultural projects, designers have commented, you miss nuance.

Visuals such as picture cards can be very helpful. Make a visual device to reduce the amount of translation. This may work very well, because it is easy to comprehend and it reduces translating time. But check whether visuals are appropriate. In a session in Co-

There are sound evolutionary social reasons as to why we are inclined more towards trust than suspicion. Otherwise, we would never have learned to cooperate on such a vast and complex scale. As a result, a large majority of us are not good at spotting liars. This has led to higher authorities, for example, being required to hold a religiously significant object, like the holy bible, while taking an oath to solemnly swear to tell 'the whole truth, and nothing but the truth, so help you God.'

The preconception may be that a young person is much easier to communicate with, but older persons usually know how to talk to people by adding or modifying questions to make the interview feel like an informal chat.

lombia, the participants, who were neighbours in a village, did not trust each other due to political conflicts. An activity was introduced to enable people to get to know each other and to express themselves freely. Participants were asked to cut pictures from magazines and place them on the forehead of a fellow participant. Each person was asked to guess who he or she was by asking questions alternately. This session turned out to be highly political, as pictures of cruel leaders were selected, which led to a tense atmosphere. Participants also did not feel confident enough to speak their minds if their position in a hierarchy was lower than that of other participants. Participants with no or low drawing skills sometimes did not feel comfortable in a drawing session. Uncertainty also led to an attitude of 'wanting to please' on the part of participants, who answered questions only to make the facilitator happy, and without sharing real thoughts and deep-seated wishes.

Stage your project - As in every design project, in the beginning you need to stage your project, which means that you develop a plan about how to approach the project: namely, when, where, and with whom do you use methods during the design process?

For a cultural study, some boundaries need to be set, because your time is limited and you cannot study everything. This is not an easy task. Which cultural groups would be relevant to study? It may be useful to first study the national culture of the targeted users, but this depends highly on your project. A region or a specific profession may be even more important and distinctive. Therefore, you need to specify the cultural context for which you design as well as the cultural background of the intended users and their most important subcultures.

Models and methods Models and methods can be used at different times in the design process. In this section, the methods are presented in a random order, with some suggestions made regarding each model and method. However, it is up to you to determine how you will use them. The next section presents some models and methods to help you get started in applying culture-sensitive design.

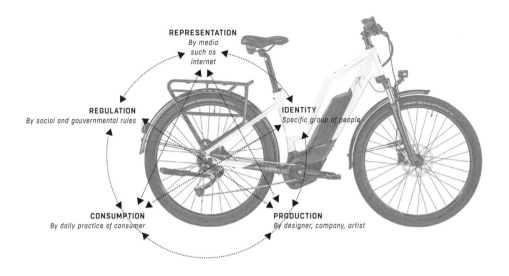

REPRESENTATION
By media
such as
internet

REGULATION
By social and gouvernmental rules

IDENTITY
Specific group of people

CONSUMPTION
By daily practice of consumer

PRODUCTION
By designer, company, artist

The circuit of culture model (after du Gay et al., 1998). More engineering-oriented designers may lose themselves in specifying the exact relationship between the processes. The arrows indicate only that processes influence each other but not exactly how.

1. Circuit of Culture model

The Circuit of Culture model can be used to explore and analyse how cultural meanings come about and how they change over time. The model demonstrates the dynamics and fluency of culture, and describes five processes that influence the cultural meaning of products. It is helpful in the study of semiotic questions about meaning rather than of normative questions concerning what is good and bad.

POSSIBLE
PROCEDURE
----
1 . Define the focus
of the study: the
phenomenon or
product category that
is relevant for the
project.
----
2. Generate relevant
questions, using the
five processes.
----
3. Study the history
of the phenomenon or
product category to
see how the meaning
has changed over
time.

What and why? Stuart Hall and other members of the British Centre for Contemporary Cultural Studies *(du Gay et al., 1997; Johnson, R.,1986)* developed this model, with the circuit being a metaphor for the interrelated processes that steer a cultural phenomenon. The model shows five processes, each of which contributes to the production of cultural meanings. Although the arrows do not indicate a specific order and hierarchy, they show that the processes are influenced by each other. The model is helpful in discussing cultural processes with stakeholders, and in developing a design vision relating to the intended cultural meaning of your design. For a better understanding, it is advised that you read the recommended literature.

When? The model can be used at the beginning of a design project to deepen the designer's understanding with respect to the meaning of a certain phenomenon, product category, or service. Each of the five processes serves as a lens to examine the development of the cultural meaning of the product over time. For a historical analysis, the model can be used to generate relevant questions as well as to structure and report findings. Insights can be used to form a solid base for the development of a design vision including the cultural meaning of the future design.

The earliest ancestors of modern mountain bikes were based around frames from cruiser bicycles such as those made by Schwinn. Riders used balloon-tire cruisers and modified them with gears and motocross or BMX-style handlebars, creating 'klunkers' used for freewheeling down mountain trails in Marin County, California.

4. Make a timeline with main findings, with text and visuals to communicate insights to project stakeholders.

- - - - - - - - - - - - - - - -

5. Use insights to develop a vision regarding the future socio-cultural meaning of your intended design.

How? A phenomenon or product related to your design project should first be chosen as a subject of study. The model can then be used to devise and to ask questions relevant for a cultural study. The insights gained from this study (analysis) can be applied to the development of a design vision (synthesis).

▶ *Production:* is the process of meaning in its creation. Products are viewed as meaningful artefacts that are produced or created by, for example, an artist, a designer, or a company. 'In this process, the company constantly seeks to take into account and respond to the ways in which consumers are 'appropriating' products' *(du Gay et al., p.59, 1997)*. Obviously, the meaning that people attribute to products cannot be fully controlled by their creators. Many factors outside the scope of designers will influence the socio-cultural meaning of things. Nevertheless, an intended meaning is useful or maybe even necessary in order to steer the design process.

Analysis: What was the intended socio-cultural meaning of an existing phenomenon or product? What meaning did the creators envisage? Synthesis: What is the socio-cultural meaning that you envisage with your design?

▶ *Consumption:* refers to the meaning-giving process through the 'consumption' or − maybe clearer − the manner in which people use products in their daily practices. This meaning-giving process is on-going; it is not influenced by the process of production but to a large extent through the people that do something with these things. The

*Use discourse
terms such as
'production' and
'representation' in
the discussion with
cultural specialists,
but do not mix
them up with
the language of
engineers.*
----
*In the design
practice, there is
limited time to do
a comprehensive
cultural study.
Nevertheless,
quick and intuitive
studies add value
to design projects.*

e-bike, for example, was created initially to support and benefit older people; it was designed as a response to a utilitarian need, but became a trendy and sporty means for workers to commute long distances between home and work. Consequently, new designs are created accommodating the needs and wishes of commuters.

Analysis: What do people practice, and how do these practices influence the meaning of the studied phenomenon or product? Synthesis: How do you think your design could or should influence the socio-cultural meaning of these practices?

▶ *Regulation:* is the process by which meaning is formed through social regulation. New products often lead to discussion and negotiation about what is acceptable and what is not. The mobile phone, for instance, has bridged the private and public context of use, which in turn has led to the development of noise-level regulations in public environments. The quiet zones in trains are an example of a design response to combat the loud and annoying conversations with which passengers were frequently confronted. Another example involves how the use of e-bikes led quickly to the need for another type of infrastructure and new traffic rules.

Analysis: What do people practice, and how do these practices influence the meaning of the studied phenomenon or product? Synthesis: How do you think your design could or should influence the socio-cultural meaning of these practices?

▶ *Representation:* refers to the influence of media on how we attribute meaning to products. Language and other media for communication, visually and orally, such as advertisements, infomercials, blogs, vlogs, tweets as well as movies, fashion, and art, influence the meaning of things and become meaningful for a particular group of people.

Analysis: What meaning of the phenomenon or product is communicated through representations in the media? Synthesis: What can you do to influence the representation of your design?

▶ *Identity:* refers to the meaning of products as an expression of people's cultural identity. In its early days, the e-bike's identity, for example, was associated with older people who were less physically active than young people. Since the e-bike is now also used (consumed) by young commuters (consumers), its identity has changed.

The meaning of things changes over time. In urbanised places, the significance of owning a car is changing slightly from being an expression of freedom and a high economic status to the restriction of a type of freedom that – owing to traffic jams and CO_2 emissions – is no longer sustainable.

Analysis: What is the meaning of the phenomenon or product in terms of identification; how does it contribute to the identification of cultural groups? Synthesis: How can your envisaged design be identified by people, for example, as part of a certain product category? What cultural group(s) will typically use your product?

2. From Persona to Cultura

POSSIBLE PROCEDURE

----

se the Cultura Question Card Set as a lens to prepare your field studies. Delineate the context by determining its boundaries and 'end users'.

Generate specific questions for each theme, and prioritise these. Search for answers in field studies, sessions with end users, and desktop research.

Structure your findings along the Cultura Canvas, and communicate and discuss the insights with your project team and other stakeholders.

POSSIBLE QUESTIONS

What social standards do people share or are dominant in the intended context?

What personal values can be identified that differ from those shared/ dominant values? What dilemmas do you observe?

Personas are representations that will be involved intentionally in the new design. They are presented as real people in order to motivate the designers and other stakeholders to empathise with them. In the process of developing such Personas, designers often learn a great deal about their intended users.

In line with this method, Chen Hao developed the Cultura method, which helps designers achieve empathy with users, not only on the basis of their individual user experiences but also on the rich insights provided with regard to the cultural context in which they live. The term Cultura was introduced by Frido Smulders, and was proposed as a new tool for designers.

What and why? Cultura is a method designed to map a specific cultural context. It involves culture-specific categories that inform designers about intended users in relationship to other people and to their material world. It aims to provide a more comprehensive view on the cultural context in which individual persons are living *(Hao, 2019; Hao et al., 2017; van Boeijen, 2015)*. The method is based on the activity theory and Hofstede's onion model *(Engeström, Y, 2001; Hofstede, 2015)*. It comes with a canvas including nine themes; these represent 'socio-cultural values' (the core of the cultural context), seven practices, and macro development. For each theme, there is a card with an explanation as well as theme-related questions that the designer or design researcher can answer. Cultura helps in gaining an empathetic understanding of a culture — especially in cross- cultural situations — and also in communicating insights to other stakeholders involved.

When? Cultura is used typically during an early stage in the design process when exploring and understanding the targeted context. Cultura can be used to generate culture-specific questions that are not only relevant for the design project but can also be used after the design research to structure findings about that context.

How? To apply Cultura efficiently, you need to carefully determine the scope of the context. This is not an easy task, and it depends highly on the project. For some projects, the scope might be very clear and specified by the client, but in others the brief is extremely broad; for example, 'design a sustainable ritual to clean teeth' is less indicative of a specific context than is 'design a sustainable ritual to clean teeth in the context of a dormitory school in Tier II city in China', which is already a more specific description. However, the reality is that products and services usually are not bound to a specific place; they either flow or are used by people in contexts that differ considerably from one another. Nevertheless, for a culture-sensitive approach, it is useful to start from a specific context. You can think of scaling up at a later stage. An advantage is that when starting from a specific context, you will gain a more profound understanding in terms of what your design might mean for people, and — the other way around — what the specific culture might mean for your design.

▶ *Macro developments:* describe contextual factors such as developments in demography, economy, and politics, including the composition of the population, geographical characteristics, development of infrastructure, and so on.

Possible questions: If you look at the bigger picture, what relevant contextual factors do you see (e.g. regarding demography, economy, infrastructure, geography, politics)? What developments are expected in the near future?

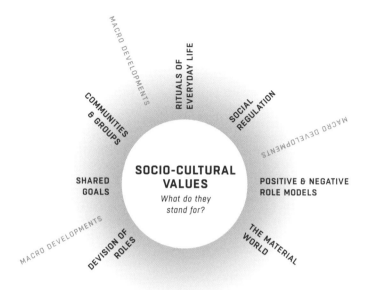

MACRO DEVELOPMENTS

RITUALS OF
EVERYDAY LIFE

COMMUNITIES
& GROUPS

SOCIAL
REGULATION

MACRO DEVELOPMENTS

SHARED
GOALS

SOCIO-CULTURAL
VALUES

*What do they
stand for?*

POSITIVE & NEGATIVE
ROLE MODELS

MACRO DEVELOPMENTS

DEVISION OF
ROLES

THE MATERIAL
WORLD

Based on personal knowledge, experience, and traditional examples, this outdoor food vendor in China has carefully designed and built his mobile kitchen on wheels. It may seem improvised and primitive, but everything has a clear function, and each detail has been carefully crafted and optimised, based on what the vendor needs in order to prepare food that fulfils his clients' wishes and expectations, and fit in perfectly with the socio-cultural values of the Chinese street-food culture.

TIPS AND
CONCERNS

The nine themes
can be used entirely
or selectively,
depending upon the
topic and the scope
of the project.

Customise your
format for data
analysis or a
checklist.

Contextual macro
factors can provide
a broader picture
of the cultural
context and the
user information.
These can include
demographics,
the economy, the
infrastructure, and
the composition
of the population,
geographical
characteristics, or
politics.

Emphasise the
insights and
inspiration rather
than the validation.

People are more
likely to offer full and
informative feedback
in return when
they know that the
designers are not
local but are trying
to understand their
culture.

Cultura cannot
be used as an
independent
evaluation tool for
your products or
services. You still
need real people in
the targeted context
in order to test
and evaluate your
design.

▶ *The material world:* is composed of artefacts (products, or things that have been designed). These artefacts, also called material culture, not only have utilitarian functions but also carry particular symbolic meanings. They have a social and cultural significance that pertains to a specific group of people or to a specific time and place.

Possible questions: What artefacts (products, services, or other things that have been designed) do people typically have or use in the intended context? What symbolic meaning or social significance do these artefacts have in people's everyday lives?

▶ *Community & groups:* is a group of people who have a shared concern or who wish to reach a goal, and interact regularly to do so. The community distinguishes who or what does or does not belong to the group. However, the scope of the community varies with different design projects. Designers need to decide how to set the border for each project.

Possible questions: How is the community defined for the project (for example, who, what where)? To which community do the end users belong? Who belongs to a specific community, and who does not?

▶ *Division of roles:* describes how duties are distributed among community members: for example, what the activities are and how they are distributed according to people's position in the hierarchy; whether it is a collective or individual activity; and division of roles by gender.

Possible questions: What roles do people have in the intended community? How are duties distributed among community members? What characterises the division of roles (e.g. gender differences, individual or collective interests, or hierarchy)?

▶ *Rituals in everyday lives:* are sequences of collective activities aimed at reaching desired ends, and that are considered to be socially essential. This also includes daily routines, special events, and activities undertaken in people's spare time.

Possible questions: What sequences of activities do people participate in (when, where, and how)? What daily routines do individuals follow (when, where, and how)? What special events do people share (when, where, and how)?

▶ *Knowing the rules:* consist of written and unwritten social agreements created by people during shared practices in order to achieve a goal. They deal with people's social relationships, and are continuously being formed and changed, reflecting the nature of the culture.

Possible questions What rules do people have when dealing with social relationships? What explicit (spoken, written) and/or more hidden (unspoken, unwritten) rules do people practice?

▶ *Role models:* represent a person (perhaps a superhero or celebrity) who is highly esteemed in the community, and who can also serve as a role model. Of course, the opposite can also exist — a negative model (devil, an enemy or anti-hero). It is even possible for a person to be seen by different parties as both hero and antihero.

Possible questions Who is highly esteemed in the community: for example, super hero or celebrity? Why? Who is held in low esteem in the community: for example, an enemy or an anti-hero? Why?

▶ *Goals of end users:* are the short- and long-term goals that users want to achieve, or personal intentions that are meaningful to them or to their community (in a specific context).

Possible questions What short-term goals do people have (individually or as a community)? What long-term goals do people want to achieve (individually or as a community)?

Kitchen tables, work tables, and coffee tables exist in all imaginable sizes and shapes according to function, available room, and needs. A table is a symbol both for meeting and eating. As opposed to a rectangular table, a round table does not enforce a hierarchically better seating position. A round table supports a form of academic or political discussion. Participants agree on a specific topic to discuss and debate. Each person has an equal right to participate.

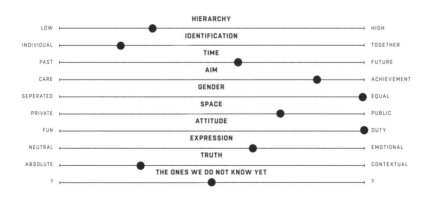

	HIERARCHY	
LOW		HIGH
	IDENTIFICATION	
INDIVIDUAL		TOGETHER
	TIME	
PAST		FUTURE
	AIM	
CARE		ACHIEVEMENT
	GENDER	
SEPERATED		EQUAL
	SPACE	
PRIVATE		PUBLIC
	ATTITUDE	
FUN		DUTY
	EXPRESSION	
NEUTRAL		EMOTIONAL
	TRUTH	
ABSOLUTE		CONTEXTUAL
	THE ONES WE DO NOT KNOW YET	
?		?

3. Socio-cultural dimensions for design

POSSIBLE PROCEDURE

Create an understanding of each socio-cultural dimension by going over their definitions and examples.

Think of other dimensions that might be relevant to the project.

Select with stakeholders the dimensions that might be important.

Make a distinction between those relevant for the design and for the design-related user research.

Generate design research questions on the basis of the selected socio-cultural dimensions.

Attune user research methods to contextual field research to anticipate possible barriers.

Use insights from contextual research to set a design direction, and apply the set to the envisaged value orientations supported by your design.

Use the set to generate product ideas.

Use the set during the design process to communicate with stakeholders and to structure insights regarding value orientations.

The set of socio-cultural dimensions (SCD) is a list along which people's orientations with regard to certain values can be considered. These value orientations steer relations between people, and they can vary on the basis of group and context. The SCD set helps designers to generate culture-specific questions, and is a useful tool to set a design direction for value orientation.

What and Why? The starting point for the use of socio-cultural dimensions is the idea that products and services mediate the relationships between people and their shared values. In principle, for example, a round table mediates an *in*formal (low hierarchy) relationship (interaction), whereas a rectangular table indicates a formal one. This is explained in Section 2. These collective values are often not explicit in either the design research or in the description of a design goal. The basic idea is that we can design for these value orientations, such as for hierarchy, gender division, or individuality, and more. The set of dimensions serves as a checklist to help in understanding current value orientations and in reconsidering how they are and could be influenced by design.

When? The dimensions can be used in various ways and during diverse moments in the design process. First of all, in an early stage, you could ask culture-specific questions about the targeted contexts and intended users. Culture-specific questions can be incorporated in the preparation of research regarding users. To examine the 'hierarchy', for example, the following questions can be asked: *'Who is the decision maker for the purchase and use of the intended product?'* or *'What products express people's social status, and how?'* Additionally, the dimensions can be used to attune the participatory and co-design methods to the local context. Furthermore, they can be implemented at a later stage to generate new ideas; for example, the hierarchy dimension could generate the question *'How can I protect an informal social situation in which power is distributed equally by design?'* Finally, they can be applied to set a design direction (intended values conveyed through design) and as a tool to reflect on preferred value orientations in cooperation; in teams and with stakeholders in the design project.

How? At first, the SCD set will serve as a checklist to determine what could be important for the design project. As with any model and checklist, however, we run the risk that it will be used superficially. it is vital to understand in the beginning what each dimension means, and to think about how this understanding can be useful in the design practice. The aim is to become sensitive with regard to possibilities rather than to fixed truths. Therefore, make sure the dimensions are applied to discuss possibilities and to rethink stereotypes. The dot in the middle can be used for communication: for example, to indicate the current and preferred situation.

▶ *Value 1. Hierarchy: (low versus high)* has to do with how power is divided within a group and the extent to which the group accepts power. Products and services mediate in this distribution of power. For example, they help people to express their social status, such as by making statues of their heroes, wearing richly decorated clothing, driving expensive cars, reading certain books, and sharing their achievements on social media, and so on. This means that you can consciously design for hierarchy. Tables in Chinese restaurants are round, for instance, and foster informal behaviour, a welcome change in a society where complying with hierarchy is important in many situations.

Example: A Dutch member of parliament travels by bike to work instead of being chauffeured in a limousine. Which values does he or she communicate? One value might be that people, irrespective of their roles in organisations, are equal when it comes to how they behave in daily situations. Another possibility is that he or she wants to communicate the importance of sustainable practices.

▸ *Value 2. Identification: (individual versus together as a group)* stands for the preferred extent of individual freedom and the tightness of the connection within a group. Do we value personal opinions higher than those of the group? What do we owe to our group members? Nowadays, in Western countries, self-expression and personal freedom are highly valued. We are no longer tied to a single group. Meanwhile, the focus on product sharing and social design is increasing. How can we deal with conflicting interests by means of design?

Example: Nokia discovered that many people in India shared their mobile phones with family members and friends. This insight resulted in the idea of incorporating a multiple contact address book application in one mobile phone, thereby making sharing easier and more comfortable.

▸ *Value 3. Time: (past-present-future)* can be approached end experienced in different ways. Some cultures value the past as something to be proud of, and they refer to their history and traditions via their practices. Others prefer to focus on the future, because, for example, they have no history to be proud of or no shared past. Some cultures approach time as being linear and monochronic (M-time, doing things sequentially) and others as being polychronic (P-time, doing things in parallel) (Hall, 1976). Furthermore, the pace of time differs from culture to culture.

Example: A Dutch manager was highly frustrated by his unsuccessful efforts to organise a Management of Change seminar with Ethiopian managers. He eventually found that he was able to capture everyone's enthusiastic support by creating a link with the history of Ethiopia's flourishing trade in the past. By making this connection, he was able to discuss challenges regarding the future (Trompenaars and Hampden-Turner, 1998). Your design could remind people of a happy past.

▸ *Value 4. The dominant aim: (care versus achievement)* underlying people's practices can differ from culture to culture. Here, groups are distinguished by the dominant values by which they seek to live. One side of the dimension is that the aim of life involves a preference for cooperation, modesty, caring for the weak, and quality of life. Society at large is more consensus oriented. The other side is a preference in society for achievement, heroism, assertiveness, and material reward for success. Society at large is more competitive.

Example: In the world of sports and games, many of them focus on achievement; examples include tennis, soccer, and smartphone applications such as Angry Birds. But there are also sports and games such as Pictionary and Twister, which focus more on social learning, interaction, and fun. Which values do you aim for in your design?

▸ *Value 5. How cultures deal with gender: (separated versus equal)* differs. In some cultures, the roles are strictly divided: men must behave in a certain way and women in another. These practices are most obvious in clothing; for instance, men wear ties and women do not. Gender sometimes also plays an important role in participatory design research: for example, when participants and facilitators are being selected (see the Introduction of this section).

Example: Baby strollers, designed as appealing products for babies and their female caregivers, are now available in sportier models that are appreciated by male caregivers. It is a relevant question to ask yourself to what extent your design will be gender neutral.

TIPS AND
CONCERNS
----
*Ensure that you are
on the same page
as colleagues and
stakeholders. Explain
what you mean with
regard to the selected
dimensions.*
----
*Values are abstract;
therefore, make sure
you have concrete
practices.*
----
*Select only the
most important
and inspiring value
orientations.*
----
*Use the Crossing
Cultural Chasms
card set for further
explanation and
examples.*
----
*The social-cultural
dimensions lens
offers a limited view
on what culture
entails.*
----
*Not all cultural
manifestations can
be explained by
cultural values, and
not all cultural values
necessarily lead
to the appropriate
manifestations.*
----
*The manner in which
people will attribute
meaning to your
design is to a large
extent beyond your
control.*

▶ *Value 6. The ways that cultures deal with personal space: (private versus public)* differ from culture to culture, depending on the population density. People in high-density areas learn to live with less personal space than those in low-density areas. In 'diffused cultures', private and professional lives are closely linked, whereas in 'specific cultures', people compartmentalise different aspects of their lives *(Lewin, 1936)*. In some cultures, playing tennis with your boss is normal, while in others it would be problematic. There are many products and services in the public environment that regulate our privacy and individual needs.

Example: With the introduction of the mobile phone, new behaviour has emerged that has subsequently led to questions about how we want to deal with each other in public spaces. New signs appear with slogans such as 'this is a silent compartment' in a train, and are intended to regulate our behaviour.

▶ *Value 7. Attitude: (fun versus duty)* refers to the extent to which a culture is more attached to a life with duties, rules, and strict norms than is another culture. Duty-oriented cultures avoid uncertainties and do not like ambiguous situations. Indulgent cultures allow the relatively free gratification of basic and natural human drives related to enjoying life and having fun. They prefer ambiguity and like to improvise. If we see products as embodying the practices of these different attitudes, we can then distinguish designs that are ambiguous and very loose in the way they can be used, and products that have clear and strict instructions on how to be used. Their 'scripts' tell us exactly what we should and should not do.

Example: Some computer programmes prescribe how we should use them, providing unambiguous and clear instructions, following a fixed order and with well-defined expected results. Other programmes give freedom to the user by offering a variety of options and leaving room for the user's own interpretation and play choices.

▶ *Value 8. Expression: (neutral versus emotional)* has to do with the appropriate way to express oneself in a culture. Should the nature of our interaction be objective and detached, or is expressing emotions acceptable? In some groups, people believe that controlling emotions is more efficient, such as when doing business; in other groups, however, showing no expression is perceived as unnatural and cold. Some people even become nervous when they feel that the group does not allow them to express themselves emotionally. Others feel embarrassed when showing emotions such as anger, because their concern is about 'losing face' in the presence of their group members'

Example: Some products evoke more emotional reactions from their users than others. In participatory design-research sessions, some cultures will be more emotionally reserved than others.

▶ *Value 9. Truth: (contextual versus absolute)* has to do with how cultures deal with truth. The cultural anthropologist Edward Hall distinguishes cultures that are accustomed to high-context communication and low-context communication. High context means that the truth of what is said depends highly on the situation: the moment in time, the people involved, the event, and other contextual factors. People accept that there is more than one reality, depending on the situation. People who are used to low-context communication tend to interpret what has been said, or communicated in another way, more as an absolute truth or statement, independent of the specific moment and situation.

Example: In traffic, people who are used to high-context behaviour might find it strange to see people waiting at a red traffic light when there is no other traffic. In contrast, people accustomed to low-context behaviour, and who are accustomed to following rules, might be annoyed when people cross against the red traffic light: in effect, changing the rules on the go.

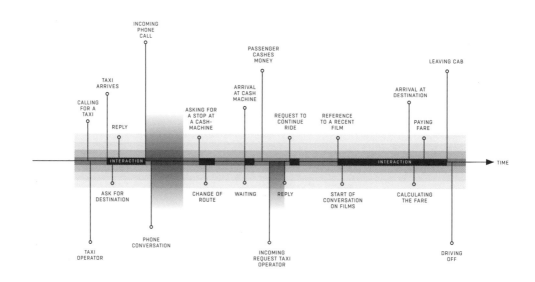

4. Role mapping

Role mapping is a method designed to help you understand intended users in relation to their cultural context. It helps you to gain an overview of the roles that a person has played at various times during his or her life, given the different contexts in which he or she lives. Insights can be used to develop a design direction.

TIPS AND
CONCERNS

The method supports
qualitative research,
and needs an
open, flexible, and
explorative mind-set
rather than one that
is mathematical in
orientation.

The onion model
template helps to
include and articulate
a person's values and
practices (symbols,
role models, rituals).

For each role (in
the flower map),
different rituals and
role models can be
identified.

The information
that people share
is personal, and
should be treated
accordingly.

Allow people to
choose what they
are willing to share.
Check and arrange
the ethical aspects
such as privacy
protection, and sign a
consent form with an
agreement.

What and why? The starting point is the idea that people have different roles during periods of their lives in diverse cultural groups, such as a daughter in a family or a director in a company. Each group comes with different roles for its members; some values and practices may stay the same, but others change over time and place. The roles can be mapped out for different reasons: To become sensitive and empathetic to the notion that people live in different cultural groups. Human behaviour as a whole cannot be described in the context of a single culture; To find where the roles overlap and where they differ or come into conflict with each other and to evaluate how products or services fit or do not fit within the scope of different roles.

When? In the first instance, role mapping can be used for yourself anytime, to help you become sensitive with respect to your own cultural context and to sharpen your lens when looking at culture. For your projects, role mapping can be used at an early stage in a design project to help you familiarise yourself with the people for whom you are designing: namely, to identify and establish your intended user group. Role-mapping templates can be used for data collection as part of an interview or context-mapping session. The outcomes are input for the development of Personas and one or more Culturas. Finally, role mapping is a useful icebreaker or introduction technique to apply when you are working with a new team. It is an easy and quick way to tell a lot about yourself and to find a common ground with your teammates.

How? Insights can be gathered through interviews, observations, desktop research, or generative sessions such as Contextmapping. The timeline and 'flower' map can be part of the sensitising diaries used in preparing Contextmapping sessions.

▸ *Timeline: Roles and Events:* Make an inventory and describe various events in the life of your intended user at a certain moment and place. In addition, state which roles the person had or still has in these events. Map the roles and event on a timeline. Where and when you start and end will depend on your project — it can be a day, a week, or over several years — and what kinds of events. And you can also take into account positive as well as negative experiences that were significant for your intended user.

▸ *Flower: Roles and Contexts:* Make a 'flower' of the roles that your intended user fulfils in in his or her daily activities. For each flower, you should also describe the context: the place, the time, and the people involved. An overall context can be included in which all roles are indicated. You can also start from a specific user group rather than from an individual person. Newly identified roles may be added to the timeline.

▸ *Reflection: Values and Practices:* Reflect with your intended user on the typical events and practices that he or she experienced in each role. What values in each of these roles and in different contexts are important to your intended user? Are there also practices for these different roles that conflict with each other in certain situations: for example, when a friend is also a colleague? For a friend, informal chats and taking time are important, whereas for a colleague, formal behaviour and efficiency are expected.

POLITICS

ECONOMY

RELIGION

SYMBOLS - Products - Artefacts
HEROES - Role models
RITUALS - Routines
Interactions - Habits - Behaviour - Art - Media - Fashion -
Representatives -
Seqnences of activities
Interactions

CULTURAL VALUES & PRACTICES

The onion model template helps to include and articulate a person's values and practices by splitting and visualising the three layers that surround and define his or her core cultural values: symbols, role models, and rituals. Select the values you think are important, and use visuals, drawings, self-made graphics, and other images.

Interactions - Habits - Behaviour - Fashion - **SYMBOLS** - Art - Media - Products - Artefacts

Representatives - **HEROES** - Role models

Seqnences of activities - **RITUALS** - Routines

5. Culture mapping with the onion model

The onion model is an easy method to map the shared values and practices of members of one cultural group, or to compare two or more cultural groups. The different layers will help you to categorise manifestations of cultural values and to think of new ones that could nurture these values. The layers might even inspire an attempt – depending on your intentions – to change current values.

TIPS AND
CONCERNS
----
*Delineation of a
context is difficult.*
----
*A more specific
way of mapping
is to select only
one socio-cultural
dimension and map
the practices that are
related. For example,
you might select
hierarchy and then
map the practices
that typically maintain
a low hierarchy;
in another map,
you might indicate
the practices that
maintain a high
hierarchy.*
----
*Use the onion model
template for role
mapping as well
as to map values
and practices that
are relevant to an
individual person.*

What and why? The onion model is a simplification of what culture entails, but it is a good tool to facilitate thinking about what it could mean in a design project. The theory of the onion model with its different layers is explained in Section 2. Since culture is comprehensive, and designers have a number of different factors they need to understand and take into account in design, many models and methods have been developed as guidelines. The onion model will help you make an inventory of relevant values and related practices.

When? The onion model is typically useful at the start of a design project as a warming-up tool or an icebreaker in participative sessions with intended users. You can also use the tool among teammates. For example, to compare each other's design backgrounds by mapping design school cultures. The model can also be used at a later stage to set your design direction and visualise your intention, answer the question as to which core values will be influenced by your design, and to generate ideas. Or, in an evaluative phase to map the intended values and practices that your design evokes or influences.

How? Discuss the layers one by one, starting with the values you think are relevant to include. For the possible value orientations, you can use the set of socio-cultural dimensions for designers.

Although the mapping session can be based on text it is better to use visuals, drawings, self-made graphics, and other images. Ask yourself: What are the *rituals* that people perform in a series of actions that are repeated over time to nurture their values? For example, the specific way in which people put their children to bed, and then end their own day. Who are the *heroes* or role models that represent or could represent the mapped values? That is someone – alive or dead, or from a movie or cartoon – that members of the group all know for his or her specific qualities. Thinking about anti-heroes might also provide insights regarding a culture. What *symbols* (customs, behaviour, artefacts, language, etc.) are associated with the values? What do the practices on each layer tell you about the values? Just mapping a few practices will help you to understand what is important to the group.

▶ *Determine the purpose of the mapping:* For example, to map current cultures, to generate questions for a cultural study, to set a design direction (intention), to generate ideas, or to evaluate concepts.

▶ *Delineate the cultural context:* where, when, and who are involved.

▶ *Copy the model as a template onto a large piece of paper:* If you are going to make a comparison, use two templates.

▶ *Map the relevant practices and values:* Do this for each layer within the chosen context, and discuss the ones that you have identified. Use text and visualisations.

▶ *Come to a conclusion:* What insights are relevant for the project?

In monochronic time cultures, activities run sequentially and are planned and limited, depending on the specific situation. In polychronic cultures, a number of activities are conducted in parallel. Aboriginals place events according to their relative importance for the individual or community in a 'circular' pattern of time. The remote community of Papunya in Australia's Northern Territory designed a Honey Ant Dreaming streetscape. For the Aboriginals, ancestral power inheres in the landscape. What happened in the past affects what happens in the present and the future. Below: Major developments in the Western, primarily linear, road and mobility infrastructures, projected along a linear timeline.

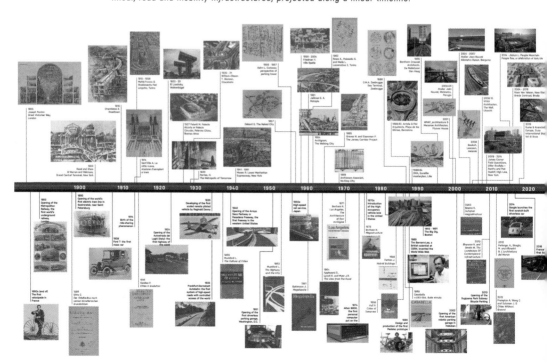

6. Timeline past-present-future

A timeline is a visual representation of the historical analysis that you can do to understand the culture for and with which you are designing. You can make a timeline of anything: for instance, a phenomenon in a specific context, such as privacy in hospitals in ...; an individual person; a soccer club in ..., a city; and so forth.

TIPS AND
CONCERNS

Timelines can be
used to sensitise
participants regarding
a certain topic to be
used in generative
sessions; see Probes
for Storytelling.

Make a timeline
together on large
sheets of paper with
pre-made cards
featuring different
characters and
subjects.

Timelines entail
visualisations that
include material
culture and support
discussion with
others.

Going far back in
history might be
time consuming and
irrelevant for your
project, so choose
your starting point
carefully.

Aim to achieve useful
insights only for
your project, since
historical analysis is
never complete, and
history hides as much
as it reveals.

What and why? Why should you, as a designer, look to the past when in fact you are in principle interested in the future? Maybe you simply want to tackle current problems and make certain changes, so why should you bother about history? The answer is that you need to know where these problems originated. Cultures are developed over long periods of time; they are intrinsically connected with history, and cannot be separated from the historical context. 'Culture includes what has 'worked' in the past' *(de Mooij, 2004, p.26)*. Therefore, a cultural study should always include some understanding of the past, otherwise – having run the risk of applying solutions that have unintended connotations – you will fail because the solutions are not aligned with the ways people deal with each other and their environment. You cannot shape a future without understanding the past and the present. At the very least, you do not have plausible arguments for your proposal. Moreover, historical insights are a tremendous source of inspiration.

The representation of insights involving a timeline helps to structure and construct a story about the past and the present, and it is a highly effective way to communicate your story to stakeholders.

When? A timeline is typically used in an early stage of the design process to facilitate understanding the cultural context and setting a design direction.

How? Obviously, you need to do a historical analysis. Depending on the topic, you can use different sources, such as the literature, observations of people and artefacts, interviews with experts or intended users, and memories of personal experiences. First delineate the context. Determine where the intervention will take place and what is needed to understand it. For a specific phenomenon – for example, 'privacy in hospitals in ...' – you could think of developments over time that influenced the way people deal with privacy in a specific place, such as the influence of technology, demographic changes, and economic and political changes. It is important to not only understand human behaviour but also to keep an eye on the material culture; for instance, what products and other artefacts are used in the specific context, and why?

You could also use the timeline for a more personal approach, such as during interviews. One designer used a hand-drawn timeline to listen to stories. The visualisation of the participant's history helped to tell the story, to point out difficulties, possible causes, successful moments, and so on. The roles that people play during their lives can also be indicated in the timeline, such as son, brother, husband, father, colleague, tourist, and so forth. This is helpful, because it shows that people live in different cultural groups and have different roles; see Role mapping in this section.

Your timeline story will be one of many possible stories. No particular one is right, but arguments based on thorough research do matter.

A versatile image of everyday life in the city of Amsterdam from past and present, made from a few of the approximately 700,000 everyday products dug up during construction of the North-South metro line. (https://belowthesurface.amsterdam)

7. Artefact analysis

Artefact analysis is a systematic examination of the meaning of things. Things are the ingredients of our material culture. We shape them and they shape us. They tell us who we are.

What and why? Designers materialise cultures. Products and services shape the way we interact with each other. They help us to tell others who we are or would like to be. Perhaps it is because of digitisation and an increasing interest in online applications that students in my design education course pay increasingly less attention to the analysis of material culture, and, in particular, to the socio-cultural meaning of form. But form is of considerable consequence for designers and the people for whom they design, both in the physical as well as in the virtual world. An analysis of artefacts helps in understanding the cultural meaning of form and in developing a direction for form.

When? Artefact analysis is useful in an early stage of the design process when an understanding of the intended users is being developed. Their material world represent the culture they are living in, and it also tells us something about where they come from; it illustrates their past. An artefact analysis can also be carried out at a later stage: for example, when a concept has been chosen, and more insights are needed in terms of how the product or service will affect the targeted cultural context.

How? For the analysis, determine the place and the time: where and when are the objects in place? Through observations — for example, home visits, transect walking (used in participatory rural appraisal approaches) in public space — 'like a fly on the wall' or a 'detective' or someone less anonymous — you can map the designed space. Capture the observed environment with pictures or movies. In the absence of humans, smart technology (sensors and cameras) can be used to observe and record what happens in human spaces. However, this raises ethical questions about what is morally acceptable in terms of privacy issues.

Recorded material in discussions with people from the examined context will be a valuable addition to your study of their culture. They are tremendous stimuli to encourage people to share their experiences, and stories. The way you approach people is of course very important. Design students who approached their intended users in an Indian village with products from a pointer booklet found out this simply did not work. The villagers were angry, because the things showed were all Western, and they did not have those things. But using products from their own environment worked well.

Some questions to be asked are: Where are things stored, used, owned? Is the space private or public? Who is the owner? What meaning do the products evoke? Do they express people's identity? What might these products tell us about the cultural context?

Findings could be used for a mapping session with the onion model; see Culture mapping in this section. You can also map them, cluster them, and find themes that are relevant for your project. You could, for example, map them on a semantic scale such as traditional versus modern; expressive versus modest; and joyful versus serious, or ask other people to map them.

New ways to gain insights are explored in Things Ethnography *(Giaccardi et al., 2016)*.

People love playing games as a means of social interaction. Shooting craps, for example, is a street game in which with a pair of dice the players make wagers on the outcome of a series of rolls. It is a popular way to meet, compete, gamble, laugh, and cheat. Successful games are always both challenging and rewarding.

Children love to depict their lives and homes in drawings, which they will be more than willing to explain in every tiny detail.

8. Probes for storytelling

There are all kinds of means that motivate people to reflect on their daily practices and to share their stories with researchers. The intention of tailor-made materials – called cultural probes – such as cards, sensitising booklets, and timelines is to encourage non-directive storytelling. With a comprehensive collection of individual and collective stories, you can build your understanding of the cultural context.

What and why? Observations and one-to-one interviews are two classic ways of gaining insights into people's everyday lives, certain phenomena, material culture, and more. Observation techniques such as 'fly-on-the-wall' – in which the observer tries to stay invisible in order to avoid influencing the situation – are often used to understand practices in the present, but they are insufficient to understand an underlying cultural meaning.

The deeper meaning relating to what people think and believe is elicited through triangulation, in which a certain phenomenon is studied in different ways. One of the first well-known anthropologists, Clifford Geertz introduced the concept of 'thick description'; this not only involves what is observed but it also describes the deeper layers that give meaning to what is observed. Storytelling is a way to reveal these deeper layers. *(Clifford Geertz, 1975)*

For the gathering of such stories, ambiguous approaches are needed. It is useful to collect people's stories and preferences concerning the topic of your interest. Questions to consider are: What is their frame of reference regarding your topic? How do they think about it? How do they act and why? Most people's stories will not be immediately ready to be told. We each have a great deal of tacit and latent knowledge that needs certain triggers – referred to as probes – to become explicit. These probes are visual and tangible means and tasks that motivate people to share their experiences. Designers construct these probes *(Gaver et al., 1999; Mattelmäki, T., 2006)*.

When? This kind of qualitative research is usually done in an early stage of the design process. Probes can be offered as a homework exercise, but they can also be used directly in semi-structured interviews, focus group sessions, and co-creation sessions. However, you can also use them in a later stage: for example, as part of a concept evaluation activity.

How? Every project needs its own probes, depending on the topic of the project, budget, time, stakeholders, and so forth; therefore, the tools for this qualitative research need to be designed. Some possibilities are listed below.

▶ *Workbooks:* are handmade booklets containing simple daily tasks, and they are usually given one or two weeks in advance to people who will be participating in interviews, focus group sessions, or co-creation sessions. The aim is to sensitise them to the topic of the session. The daily exercises are customised invitations to share experiences. The timeline for 'one day in …' with the question to highlight daily activities and moods is often included. Participants who are not used to these kinds of assignments and to doing homework – for example, if they are illiterate – will not be able to fill in the booklets. They may feel comfortable talking but not writing down their thoughts. And for some people, a diary makes no sense, because their daily activities are always the same. In these situations, the booklets can be used not as an exercise to be completed ahead of time but to be filled in together with the participants in a session.

There was a time when the word 'avatar' meant the earthly manifestation of a god. But since the earliest days of the Internet, an avatar has come to mean one's digital self. In a role-playing video game, the player controls the actions of a self-designed character who can attain victory by completing a series of quests or by reaching the conclusion of a central storyline. Nowadays, people are often accustomed to switching rapidly between virtual worlds, cultures, and identities.

Graphic diaries can present everyday life experiences in surprisingly personal and meaningful ways. Like the graphic diaries by industrial designer Dwinita Larasatii, some of which have been published.

'The viewing process is a dynamic interaction between the photographer, the spectator and the image; meaning is actively constructed, not passively received'. (Donna Schwartz, 1989)

▶ *Photo and video elicitation:* is a well-known method used in ethnography. Design researchers use the camera to capture the targeted context, but intended users are also asked to take photos and/or to make videos recording elements in their daily lives. Mobile applications such as WhatsApp and WeChat can be used to ask people to send a picture with a short explanation in text about a certain topic. For generating questions and tasks, open and ambiguous questions work best; for example, for a project about commuters having breakfast on the go, the question *'What summarises your breakfast experience best?'* will lead to richer answers than the task *'Take a picture of your breakfast'*. Afterwards, the design researcher and the participant need to discuss together the meaning of what is in the pictures and the video.

P'hotographs are 'polysemic', capable of generating multiple meanings in the viewing process.' (Roland Barthes, 1964)

▶ *Cards:* with images and a short text to explain the main topic that the image also represents trigger storytelling. There are different types. *Cultural cards* trigger stories about daily practices and important values; *topical cards* elicit stories that focus on the design topic; *option cards* help in understanding participants' preferences by sorting and ranking them; *interview cards* guide semi-structured interviews; and *timeline cards* help participants describe a day in their lives. Moreover, cards can motivate people to talk when used as a game element: for example, when turning them over one by one as in a memory game, or when playing with them as in a family game.

▶ *Preference booklets:* consist of two sets of images in two booklets to be used in an interview session. The images in one booklet are ordered 'abcde', and in the other one the images are ordered in the opposite way, 'edcba'. Two images − one from each booklet − are shown to the participant, who is asked to select the one he or she prefers, followed by a discussion about the reasons for the selection. After the discussion, the researcher will turn to the next page, and the selection and discussion starts again, and so on. The advantage of this probe is that participants can react or respond to something specific, which is sometimes easier than starting with a more open question. Use of the booklets created an informal atmosphere, letting the participants think out loud, sharing their considerations.

▶ *Products and prototypes:* can also serve as excellent probes to learn about people and their cultural context. To predict the underlying meaning and consequently the acceptance of a new design, for example, it is useful to know what might be Most Advanced, Yet Acceptable (MAYA) *(Loewy, 1963)* in the targeted culture. Concrete examples help intended users to provide feedback and share their stories, such as in a product confrontation session. Therefore, three-dimensional artefacts can be used for more than just usability tests in an early stage of the design process.

▶ *Role-playing:* helps to lower the barrier to sharing opinions, and it also helps design researchers to experience people's lives if the people play out certain situations themselves. In generative sessions, participants can be placed in a specific role, such as that of an actor or a television presenter. A simple television or computer frame is then the probe that stimulates storytelling. Other attributes such as a microphone, hats, and other wearable items help to bring the stories to life.

▶ *Games:* are not designed only for entertainment but also to persuade people to behave in a healthy and positive way. Furthermore, games can be used to stimulate storytelling. There is considerable literature on the topic of game design. The cookbook method paper gives a complete and useful overview on how to design such a persuasive game *(Siriaraya et al., 2018)*. Just using certain elements from existing games will be helpful as well.

The Chinese government is experimenting with a social credit system that is called an attempt to promote 'reliability' in society and the economy. Credit software, managed by Jack Ma's online store empire Alibaba, provides access to the data of more than 1 billion users of the Alipay mobile payment app. High scorers enjoy a whole range of extras. In essence, the system uses technology to enforce existing legal prohibitions through a socio-cultural system that respects hierarchy, obedience, and commonality, which in most cases are valued as virtues. People in China are encouraged to adopt this system with the promise that it will improve their society.

9. Contextmapping in cross-cultural situations

Contextmapping is the name of a systematic method created to collect rich, qualitative data about targeted design contexts often focused on intended users. With the help of generative tools and a step-by-step procedure, participants are encouraged to share their experiences and thoughts.

Asian people often are more reserved with regard to expressing their opinions and emotions due to strict hierarchical relationships. In ancient Chinese society, for instance, the Emperor controlled everything by dictating rules and orders that everyone had to obey. The second most important people were the nobles and government officials. Third in line came the farmers, who had the poorest occupation at the time but still ranked above the artisans. Merchants, who often became so wealthy that they were considered a threat to the Emperor and nobles, had the lowest status (just above slaves) because they did not produce anything and profited from others.

What and why? Because the contextmapping method does not explicitly address culture-specific aspects of people's lives, the Cultura communication toolkit has been developed. Contextmapping is included in the present book, however, because it is the foundation of the Cultura process. The importance of attuning the method to different cultural groups is crucial.

Contextmapping was originally developed at Delft University of Technolgy, building on Liz Sanders' work on generative techniques, described in detail in the book Convivial Toolbox *(Sanders & Stappers, 2012)*. The method helps designers to tap into people's latent and tacit knowledge. Several probes – discussed in the section on probes for storytelling – are used in the contextmapping process. However, studies have shown that contextmapping – especially in non-Western countries – does not always work as intended. East Asian participants, for example, found it difficult to handle the ambiguity of generative tools. Compared to the average Western participants in such sessions, they were more reserved with regard to expressing their opinions and emotions, or relating anecdotes. Making a collage, which is part of the contextmapping process, was often not within their comfort zone.

When? Contextmapping is most beneficial in a project's pre-concept stage, when there is still considerable latitude for finding new design opportunities. It fits well in co-design or co-creation processes as well as in multi-stakeholder projects. The contextmapping starting point is the idea that designers are experts in the design process, whereas the people they design for are regarded as experts in the context of their individual experiences in everyday life.

How? The contextmapping process usually consists of a series of activities that are divided roughly into two phases: collecting user insights and communicating them. During these phases, designers can implement several research methods, such as interviews, observations, generative tools, and certain elements from cultural probes. The number of participating users is usually small, ranging from three to 20 people.

Possible procedure The Delft Design Guide provides a general description. Highlighted below are the steps that need extra attention owing to possible cultural differences.

▶ *Planning:* In cross-cultural situations, more time than expected is often needed, especially if you are working in rural areas in non-Western countries. The pace of living is slower than in highly industrialised countries, and time based on the natural cycle from light to dark and dark to light (diurnal rhythms) might be more important than time according to the clock.

▶ *Preconceptions:* You will have your own opinions and ideas with regard to every study. Extra attention should be given to what your expectations are with respect to the targeted people and the context. A way to sensitise yourself to cultural biases is to map your expectations about the targeted context in an infographic and reflect on them in a later stage.

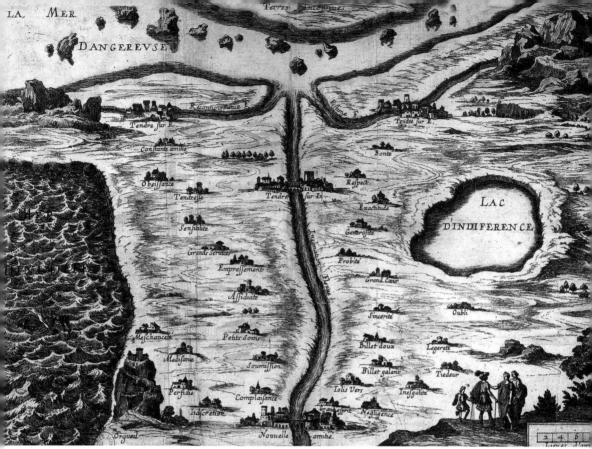

The enormously popular 'Carte du pays de Tendre' (Map of the Land of Tenderness) was conceived as a social game in the mid-17th century by Madelaine de Scudery, and came to symbolise the politically and culturally independent, aristocratic salonnières (women who hosted salons). It shows various routes towards love along 'the river of inclination', 'the lake of indifference', and a web of villages named 'love letter' and 'little trinkets'.

Family lineage is very important within Chinese culture. On the Shanghai Marriage Market, parents search for a suitable partner for their child, using age, height, job, income, education, family values, Chinese zodiac sign, and personality as matching standards. Their children, however, prefer popular dating apps like Tantan and Momo.

TIPS AND
CONCERNS

First reflect on
yoFirst reflect on
your own cultural
background with
regard to the topic
of your project; what
are your underlying
beliefs, values, and
practices?

Never forget a
designer's inherent
strength: the ability
to visualise findings
and thoughts. It is a
tremendous help in
communication.

Sensitising tasks can
have different forms.
Workbooks in the
form of diaries do
not always work as
intended; see Probes
for Storytelling. Be
sure to design the
appropriate form.

▶ *Preliminary study:* Study the targeted context through desktop research and interviews with experts. Study the topic of your project first in a familiar context in order to have a frame of reference and to be able to compare when examining the targeted context. This helps to avoid the automatic 'everything that is new is because of the other culture' reflex. It will be easier to see people's practices based both on universal principles of human behaviour and on ones that are typical for the cultural context.

▶ *Selection of participants and facilitators:* Select them carefully. In some cultures, people will not speak up readily in the presence of anyone with a higher social status (e.g. employer, village chief, and so on) or — for women — when men are around. Consider having sessions with children. They are often less sensitive to the cultural codes, and are therefore more free to express themselves than adults.

▶ *Sensitising tasks and session material:* Make sure that they are attuned to the local culture. Think of the duration of tasks, language, style, whether online or offline, and so forth.

▶ *Ethics:* Use ethical procedures to check what should be done to protect people's privacy, safety, and well-being.

▶ *Sessions:* Record the session and/or make notes. An open mind and an authentic interest are essential. Take time to get to know each other. Materials such as presentation slides, templates, and collage materials should be appropriate as regards people's values.

▶ *Transcripts, clusters, themes:* Use qualitative analysis approaches, but, if the budget and other factors allow, involve local people in the interpretation of results.

▶ *Communication:* The communication with other stakeholders in the project needs additional contextual information in order for the meaning of what people say to be fully understood; see From Persona to Cultura.

Cultural ignorance can have deadly consequences. Insider conflicts known as 'green-on-blue' attacks have killed at least 45 international troops in Afghanistan. Samples from the 28-page Brochure for Understanding the Culture of Coalition Forces: 'If a coalition soldier asks you about your family members, including your wife or daughter, do not take this as an offense or an attempt to humiliate you. If a coalition solider is excited or wants to show appreciation for your work he may pat you on the back or shoulder. It is not meant as an insult and you should not take it personally.'

The familiar response from artists like Beyoncé who are criticised for tokenisation or appropriation, is that they were simply drawing inspiration. But it often seems no one wants to engage with those parts of a culture that do not involve appealing outfit options. When done well, a taste for other cultures has its advantages.

10. Observation

TIPS AND
CONCERNS
----

*Do not base your
understanding of
a culture on the
observations of only
a few individuals.*
----
*Everything that is
new for you is not
necessarily specific
to the culture.*
----
*Watch out for
'looking for what you
expect to see'.*
----
*People may adjust
their behaviour
because of your
presence.*
----
*A safe and easy-to-
reach place could
lead to you missing
somewhere more
relevant.*
----
*Observe the material
culture around
the interviewee or
observed person, and
try to understand
the socio-cultural
meaning of things
relating to that
culture.*
----
*Designers are
not pre-eminently
trained experts in
observing cultures.
Yet sometimes they
need to experience
the new context
first-hand in order to
really understand the
context.*

Observation is a classic method to actively acquire information about a phenomenon from a primary source. Designers typically use various lenses to look at people. One is the ergonomic lens when studying people and their relationship with products regarding universal needs such as usability, comfort, and safety. Another lens is the cultural lens, as described throughout this book.

What and why? The method of observation requires the use of all the senses. Examine a larger whole without influencing it, as opposed to interviews or participatory sessions whwre this is inavoidable. Cultural observations are qualitative and descriptive, but they can be quantitative by adding numerical values to the observed phenomenon by counting or measuring.

When? Observations are a great help in an early stage in order to gain a deeper understanding of an unknown or little-known context. If you already have a certain understanding of the target group culture, use them to evaluate your premises and recognise cultural factors. In a later stage, prototypes can be evaluated through observations: In each of these stages, it is important to take several aspects into account: With a new culture – starting to understand the culture; With a known culture – recognising cultural factors; When evaluating ideas, concepts, and final designs – finding out how people understand the design.

How? Basic understanding should be obtained from literature, experts and websites.

▶ *Prepare:* by learning something about basic local habits, such as taking off your shoes. Do this by asking someone from that culture explicitly about what to say, wear, or do, and what not to say, wear, or do. This will avoid a bad start. If you want to observe people unnoticed in real-life situations, you need to know whether and how you might be noticed. Sensitise yourself with respect to possible differences of value orientation by doing research on values and practices regarding communication.

▶ *Use data collection:* Use photos, ecetches of situations, videos, or audio recordings if allowed, and only if these media convey the real message. If people begin behaving differently because of a camera, or only say socially acceptable or politically correct things, use another approach. Templates for taking notes are useful if you know in advance which aspects are important. Or ask people to collect observational data themselves: for instance, by asking them to take pictures of their environment.

▶ *Evaluation:* The value of your observation will be determined in dialogue with those being observed and other experts from the observed context. The collected materials and data can be used in interviews to develop further comprehension by using them as probes to stimulate storytelling in participatory sessions. Another way to process data from observations is to make a visual essays; small booklets containing pictures accompanied by short explanations of what is being identified. Such booklets are a tremendous source of inspiration and a means for discussion in a design team.

Videotelephony on smartphones can feel like two people are talking while checking their email, which feels far remote from anything close to the art of conversation. Face Time Attention Correction adjusts the set of your eyes so that it looks like you are making eye contact, even when you are not looking at the camera. It is both a technical marvel and an unsettling confirmation that the post-reality age is officially here.

As optimistic as AT&T may have been when they began to develop the videophone in 1964, even they could not have imagined that 60 years later it would be on portable devices in the hands of approximately 2.5 billion people worldwide.

11. Interviews

Interviewing involves face-to-face consultations aimed at collecting data about people's expertise, opinions, beliefs, experiences, and so on. As with observation, designers use various lenses. Even though general descriptions of interviewing as a data collection method can easily be found, a few extra points regarding a cultural lens need to be highlighted.

What and why? Interviews are usually directed by an interviewer who asks questions in a structured or semi-structured way. The topics can be anything, as long as they are acceptable to the interviewee. Interviews can result in a more in-depth understanding, not only with regard to opinions and user needs but also to people's cultural background. More than in observations, you can steer what kind of data will be gathered. For the purpose of understanding a socio-cultural context, you will need semi-structured and fairly open questions that do not control the direction too much. The aim is generally to collect rich data in the form of stories that will 'paint the cultural picture'.

When? At the start of a design project they can help to gain an initial understanding of a culture. Some people are proud of their culture and are eager to talk about it, while others may be critical of it. In a later stage, concepts can be evaluated by means of interviews. You can find out whether you have succeeded in the cultural appropriation of your design or identify unintended mismatches. Using interviews in combination with observations can be repeated multiple times in iterative steps for participatory sessions where people can share their ideas. The main goals are to understand the culture; recognising cultural factors and valuate ideas, concepts, and final designs.

How? Prepare by learning a few basic norms and values for communication. You need to make people feel safe and to have a genuine interest in them. Ask them explicitly about what to say, wear, or do, and what not to say, wear, or do.

▸ *Sensitise* The gap between high-context versus low-context communication may raise the question of how do you interpret what is said: should it be literally or do you also have to pay attention to contextual factors such as body language. Do you also 'listen to the air'? If you do, you might want to reconsider the value of making textual transcripts. If you do not share a common language, it is impossible to interview people and you wel need an interpreter. Select someone whom your participants trust, and who both understands the aims of your research and your cultural/professional background. Let them know in advance that you are also interested in tiny details that rmay eveal the implicit. You can also use probes for storytelling like pictures.

▸ *Data collection* Explain your goals and intentions and ask for permission to use the data, take pictures, make videos, or use audio recordings. Consider conducting the interview together with a team member to divide tasks. If circumstances allow, try to conduct interviews in a context that is natural for the interviewee.

▸ *Evaluation* Recorded material can be transcribed and analysed together with others: for example, by cluster analysis. Quotes can be used to illustrate findings when discussing insights with stakeholders.

In Bangladesh, most people drink water drawn from shallow tube wells that were installed in the 1970s to end the use of microbially unsafe surface water. Bangladesh suffers significantly from naturally occurring arsenic in groundwater.

A smart water supply system

Currently, an estimated 32 to 77 million people in Bangladesh suffer from overexposure to arsenic through drinking water. Arsenic is a metalloid, which in nature is commonly found in soils. Rivers flowing from the Himalayas contain sediments that are deposited in, among others, the lower deltaic areas of Bangladesh, where, under strong reducing conditions, the arsenic dissolves in the groundwater.

In Bangladesh, most people drink water drawn from shallow tubewells that were installed in the 1970s to end the use of microbially unsafe surface water. When consumed in large quantities over an extended period the arsenic contamination can result in serious health risks such as skin lesions, edema, gangrene, black foot disease, and malignant diseases like skin, bladder, and lung cancer. Designer and researcher Annemarie Mink began work on this problem by starting discussions with water companies, governments, NGOs, institutes and locals. The systems often provide an intermittent supply caused by lack of maintainance, necessary disinfection, filter replacement. Or suffer from low water pressure, and leakage. Paying for a commodity like water is also problematic, which is often seen as 'a gift from God'. The difference in taste and temperature between groundwater and piped water is another obstacle, so people use piped drinking water mainly for showering, toilet flushing and cleaning. This all reduces trust in the water quality and supply, and in the system operator.

Servive system While engineers took on the task of developing a more affordable filter system and improving the water's taste and temperature, the main challenge was to develop the service to make the water supply system trusted, accessible, and acceptable. As access to mobile services in Bangladesh is rapidly increasing, using a smartphone app for operation and maintenance seemed a logical way of improving system. To do so, a deeper understanding of the local culture was needed, including factors such as hierarchy, literacy, smartphone ownership and usage, the socio-economic situation, religion, and the health situation. By means of interviews, questionnaires, focus-group sessions, workshops, and co-creative sessions, involved stakeholders from different regions in Bangladesh became active participants in finding an appropriate solution. This resulted in a smartphone app that can be used to link the system operators and the families using the water supply system. The operator can use the app to test the local water quality and

Water is our most basic requirement. Water metaphors define the flow of our thoughts and time. Great cultures have historically all developed and flourished around rivers and access to the sea. The use of water clocks dates back to the Old Babylonian period (circa 2000 BC-1600 BC). The image shows the 14th century hydraulic Dar al-Magana water clock in Fes, Morocco.

Payment distribution is still a problem in Bangladesh. Most people want to pay per amount of water (a fair distribution of the costs for your water use), but that leads to 'illegal ticking' and tampering with water meters ... .' (Annemarie Mink, 2019)

submit the outcomes to a database that can be monitored. He can also provide information about supply issues and the time it takes to resolve them and assists in the payment for drinking water. For the water consumer, the app includes the possibility of discussing water quality with other consumers. In addition, it contains a teaching package designed to inform the users about the service and water-related health issues. Video, drawings and spoken messages make it accessible for non-literate users.

Bangladesh has a good 3G network with coverage in even the smallest villages. Almost all households own at least one phone, of which around 30% are smartphones. Rural families in Bangladesh use these for communication, sharing pictures, playing games, and browsing the Internet for information. Family ties are a significant aspect of the Bangladeshi culture, and the phone is an important means of staying in touch with family and friends. Children borrow their parents' mobile phone to help do their homework. Even illiterate people are able to grasp the mobile phone functionalities they desire to use.

The meaning that the form of the design communicates should resonate with the user's expectations and desires. Regular feedback on prototypes from intended users is essential in order for the resulting design to be accepted.

In order to increase the likelihood of acceptance of the app various factors needed to be considered. For example, Annemarie hesitated to use gamification elements, because adults had said that drinking water was a serious topic that should not be approached in a playful manner. In addition, the main water users and collectors are women, while the phone owners are often men. Women feel uncertain about using a smartphone. This attitue is changing, and can be addressed by developing a user Interface in a smart way and that keeps notice of all cultural and social restrictions that matter.

Designing hospital Beds

NPK is an established design agency in the Netherlands. Among other things, they design hospital beds in different countries and for different clients.

The design agency usually follows a fairly systematic design process, with pre-defined phases and deadlines, and with an estimated hourly budget. Part of the process involves a list of requirements that the designers agree on with the client, and that serves as an important starting point to fall back on during the design phase. Consequently, the designing process is often approached from the inside out, which means that first the technical structure, based on technical and ergonomic requirements, is determined. The outer part, the visual appearance, is designed in detail in a later stage. However, different contexts ask for different approaches.

'They keep you busy forever until they think it is good enough. This is very different from how we do it here.' (Jos Oberdorf, 2019)

Person-driven: an outside-in approach In a project with a client in Turkey, the process went differently. Payment was based on a fixed number of hours, and dependent on an estimation of how much the company was willing to pay. It occurred in instalments, and since the last one was to be paid at the end of the project, the design agency depended greatly on the company director's decisions. In this case, the director's personal opinion was paramount. He followed every step in the design process and made decisions on every aspect of the design. And although the designers made several sketches, which took many more hours than expected, the client was still not able to arrive at a decision. It was only during the process that the designers realised that not only were the primary functions led by the director but also the style preference; a German-style hospital bed. The designers also became aware that the sketches needed to communicate the visual appearance more clearly than they had been accustomed to presenting, because non-designers cannot understand everything from sketches. Once the new process was clear, it was easier to conclude the project.

Product-driven: an inside-out approach In a project involving Dutch hospital beds, the process went as expected; everything was clear and written down in a list of requirement in advance. The designers started with mood boards to facilitate understanding the final form and to experience the 'look and feel' of the end design. They followed a product-driven, inside-out approach, in which the functional parts (mechanisms, materials, technical working principles) were specified first, followed by prototyping and testing. After that, renderings of the possible final form were made. In this manner, the designers went gradually from an abstract definition of the product requirements, through the functional parts, to the final form. The project was on budget, because everyone knew exactly what to do, and they were on the same page as the client as regards the decision-making process.

Process-driven: an iterative approach In a project involving Indian hospital beds, the process was unexpectedly very structured. It started with extensive field research, with doctors, nurses, and patients and their families involved. In the beginning, it was new to the doctors to involve the practices and experiences of nurses, but they were very cooperative and open to the agency's approach. Differences emerged especially regarding the design itself because of the different health care system and contexts, such as rural versus urban; home care versus hospital care; governmental versus private and premium care; and the absence of homes for the elderly. Consequently, the requirements as regards hospital beds in India are different from the type of hospital bed needed in the Netherlands. One design would not fit all situations. In

While the Vietnam War was raging in 1969, John Lennon and his wife Yoko Ono used the bed as a symbol of peace in a nonviolent form of protest against war. The Lennons invited the press and like-minded artists to join them in bed in order to stir up attention. When asked if he thought the Bed-In had been successful, Lennon replied: 'It's part of our policy not to be taken seriously. Our opposition, whoever they may be, in all manifest forms, don't know how to handle humour. We are humorous.'

'With this client, it was very easy to have that discussion, to level. Before even one line was drawn, we knew where we were heading.'
(Jos Oberdorf, 2019)

Dutch hospitals, there are wide corridors to accommodate beds with patients being moved around, while in India it is the employees who move, not the beds with the patients. Furthermore, the body length of the Indian population is shorter. Dutch hospital beds need to be two metres long and sometimes need a bed-extender, which allows increasing the length by up to 20 centimetres. Indian hospital beds only need to be 170 centimetres in length, which fit 95 percent of the Indian population. So far so good; but unexpectedly, in a later stage of the project, the client asked for an extra design, especially for home care. This had not been budgeted for, but the client insisted. As a result, and similar to the Turkish approach, the project was unable to be finalised until the client decided.

Role of culture-sensitive design In reflecting on the three different experiences, Jos concluded that culture sensitivity means that right from the start you need to find out who has the design leadership. Is it you or is it the client? Who runs the project? Who makes the decisions, and how are they made, based on what criteria? How is the hierarchy organised? Therefore, open discussions with the client are needed to understand each other's perspectives. All stakeholders must be involved, and it is essential to balance all their different needs. These requirements – though most of the time hidden – have to be made explicit.

MEANING AND IMPACT

DESIGNS
IN CONTEXT

This section discusses a collection of designs from the real world. The aim is to show with a variety of topics how products, under the influence of developments in societies, play their role in cultural processes. Together, they provide a picture of our designed world and how it acquires meaning in different contexts.

Miguel de Cervantes published Don Quixote in two parts, in 1605 and 1615. It is one of the world's most influential cultural
achievements, and is a founding work of Western literature. Don Quixote fails to see the world for what it is, preferring to imagine
that he is living out a tale of mediaeval chivalry. As a reader, you may consider yourself smarter than Don Quixote, but as soon as
you think you understand something, Cervantes introduces something that contradicts your premise.

MAKING A DIFFERENCE

Culture-sensitive design is not only about differences in nationalities and customs; above all, it is about designers being conscious of cultural borders and differences so that they are able to come up with better and innovative designs. The focus on opportunities for design is more relevant than avoiding mismatches. Paramount here are cross-cultural fertilisation, resourcefulness, imagination, and liberation from learned opinions, prejudices, and judgements.

People analyse and interpret reality on the basis of constructed cultural models. The figure of Don Quixote represents the hidden essence of human culture: the centrality of heroic madness and its related death anxiety in all people. It concerns the flimsy, delusional nature of the things that grant humans conviction and self-aggrandisement, and the ironic, and ultimately tragic, need to acquire this conviction and self-aggrandisement to experience the goodness, richness, and reality of life. The phrase 'tilting at windmills' to describe an act of attacking imaginary enemies or an act of extreme idealism derives from an iconic scene in the book.[11]

To gain insight into the importance of culture-sensitive design, we need to take a close look around the world in terms of how design has developed over a longer period of time. The most convincing and educational examples are, by definition, those designs that have proven themselves in practice – ones that survive for long periods, remain successful, keep adapting to changing circumstances, and seem able to evolve. Good designs are also characterised by their ability to function as a vessel for diverse cultural interpretations and meanings.

In this section, the designs selected have proven their cultural significance in the real world, and they all share a culturally sensitive component. The world as a whole is involved, and the designs are products of the past hundred years, relevant for young and old alike. The perspective, the nature, and the impact differ from one example to the other.

The medium is the message The Canadian philosopher Herbert Marshall McLuhan (1911-1980), with his visionary ideas about the role of media, was a harbinger of what we now call the digital revolution. As early as 1959 he wrote about the concept of a 'global village'. More than 30 years before it was invented, McLuhan predicted the World Wide Web. His conceptual framework was comprehensive, and his view on how media would change society was fundamental, as summarised in his famous quote, *'the media is the message'*. As an example, he uses the invention of electricity (technology) and the lamp (design). In contrast to sitting around a fire, which is bound by time and place, we can use the light as a medium: for example, to signal (on/off), read, play games in the evening, and create ambiance.

The core is not all those activities, according to McLuhan, but the fact that we become detached from time and place, from sunrise and sunset, and from where we are. We become less dependent on the collective and can act in a much more individual fashion, which in turn leads to diversity. At the same time, however, we become detached from the human aspect and veer into an all-encompassing system of digital information. This was an early reference to what the Internet is doing to us now. Remarkably, McLuhan found already in 1964 that we humans are fascinated by what he referred to as 'own extensions': namely, responding to peer pressure, threats, or fear of threats. And in order not to become intoxicated by this – namely, undergoing a global information flow and walking behind like a headless chicken – according to McLuhan we must become immune and distance ourselves. Artists can help with this, because, ideally, they think, feel, and act in a liberated manner, regardless of all kinds of practical interests.

McLuhan contends that all media have a compelling influence on humans and society. Every aspect of Western mechanical culture has been shaped by print technology, but our modern age is the age of electronic media.

McLuhan described key points of change in how humans viewed the world, and how these views have been changed by the adoption of new media. He wrote, 'The technique of invention was the discovery of the nineteenth century', brought on by the adoption of fixed points of view and perspective by typography, 'while the technique of suspended judgment is the discovery of the twentieth century', brought on by the bard abilities of radio, movies and television.

McLuhan's work shows that both the technical invention and the design were already embedded in our global culture, otherwise he could not have noticed and predicted that. This fact also confirms the above notion that cultural developments arise from their own dynamics, which are not designed, and therefore lie outside the domain of every designer. The design process does not lead, but follows technological and cultural developments. And the social consequences fall within a fixed palette of human behaviours and emotions that are embedded in our nature (genetic codes). This palette in turn translates into adapted learned standards and actions that we agree with, share, and pass on from young to old in the form of our culture, and are expressed in practical and aesthetic codes.

Personal computer and the Internet To date, the personal computer and the Internet have had the greatest influence on almost all cultures worldwide. Throughout human history, innovations for communication – such as writing, the printing of books, the telephone, and television – have had a significant impact on cultures. Every innovation has called for new forms of behaviour and possibilities that challenged old cultures to adapt. And, as often happens with something new, in the beginning these innovations have not been well understood. The Greek philosopher Plato, for example, warned against the dangers of writing and reading. He denounced writing as being detrimental to intellectual development, warning that – in terms of the transmission of knowledge – people would stop exercising their own memory of the information because they would rely on what was written. The invention of the printing press was also seen as a threat to European culture, social order, and morality. 'Since they started practicing this perverse excess of printing, the church has been massively damaged', complained Francisco Pen-

Smartphones have become the lens through which we view life. With an estimated one third of millennials experiencing live events largely through their phones, people seem more focused on sharing an experience than enjoying it.

na, a Dominican defender of the Spanish Inquisition. Similar concerns have also arisen during the emergence of more recent innovations, such as the introduction of a type of train that would run much faster than is considered good for people's health. Likewise, in some still existing subcultures television is viewed as having a pernicious influence. The mobile phone was seen as an unnecessary addition in the 1990s because most people already had an answering machine at home. It was impossible to imagine that the culture of everyday life would become so interwoven with the Internet.

The flourishing of online dating is another striking example of how social media influences behaviour and vice versa, as its use leads to new forms of being together, with all the advantages and disadvantages. The Internet also became a platform for shopping and online learning as well as for political parties, for accelerated revolutions such as the Arab Spring, and for violent groups such as terrorists, and not to forget the porn industry. Young people were quick to discover social media, and that has had a major cultural impact on their activities, such as the way they deal with time and privacy, their appearance, their use of language, their manners, and, not least, the way they deal with parents or caregivers. The full potential of the Internet was only fully discovered when what used to be a possibility became a real need – a way to survive. We saw, for example, that a connection to the Internet became a lifeline among refugee migrants. The current coronavirus crisis is now driving people worldwide to turn to the Internet for education and to maintain contact with others. We do not know yet how this major event will change cultures both locally and globally, but it seems that the impact on cultures will be extensive. And will even become more evident in cultures that did not go along with the change.

Nelson Mandela and Trevor Baylis holding the first model of the Freeplay wind-up radio. Its success spread throughout Africa, helping people to gain access to all kinds of vital information on healthcare issues via radio broadcasting. The photo shows Maasai women in Kenya listening to a later model of the Freeplay radio.

'We now have cultural machines so powerful that one singer can reach everybody in the world, and make all the other singers feel inferior because they're not like him. Once that gets started, he gets backed by so much cash and power that he becomes a monstrous invader from outer space, crushing the life out of all the other human possibilities.'
(Alan Lomax 1915-2002)

An iconic radio Trevor Baylis (1937-2018), a physical training instructor, engineer, stuntman and, at 45, full-time inventor in London, had a special interest in the care of disabled people. In his work as a stuntman, he was exposed to the needs of disabled people as a result of seeing colleagues who had been injured. After seeing a documentary in 1991 about the enormous AIDS epidemic in rural parts of Africa, and especially the difficulty of providing information about safe sex, he had the innovative idea of developing a wind-up radio. Radio technology was expensive, especially in underdeveloped regions without reliable electricity where people had to depend on batteries. Batteries were not affordable, not available in rural areas and also not sustainable, since there was no recycling system.

Inspired by his grandmother's wind-up gramophone, Trevor designed a robust, manually powered radio that would function without batteries. The first prototype could play for 14 minutes, and was powered by the user turning a crank. This stored energy in a spring, which then powered an electrical generator. Thanks to his new design being featured on BBC's Tomorrow's World programme, and to an interview on the World Service, Baylis found investors who helped him to manufacture the radio in South Africa's Cape Town, where he started a production unit that employed disabled people.

The vast majority of these early-production radios were sold to aid agencies to be distributed freely. And although the radio was quite heavy in comparison to other mobile radios, people recognised its quality and embraced the story of supporting people in need. Over time, the radio became very popular among consumers who could afford radios, and eventually the Freeplay radio could be sold for profit as well. When Baylis's design was manufactured as the BayGen Freeplay radio, it won him the 1996 BBC Design Awards for Best Product and Best Design, turning it into an iconic piece of British design, featured in the United Kingdom Science Museum collection. Spin-offs of this design included a wind-up torch and mp3 player, along with shoes that generated enough electricity from the wearer's movement to charge a mobile phone. The distribution of the millions of dirt-cheap, wind-up radio sets ultimately contributed to the important turning point in the AIDS epidemic,

A telenovela is a type of TV series from Latin America, also known as teleserye (Philippines), dorama (Japan), téléroman (Quebec), or dramas (rest of Asia and the Middle East). Authorities have used the medium frequently to transmit socio-cultural messages by incorporating them into storylines. Mexico used them successfully to introduce the idea of family planning.

Telenovelas are booming in East Africa, but are not produced locally. They are imported from Latin America and dubbed into local languages. Most cable companies have at least one telenovela channel. Billboards promote them and they are on TV in restaurants and government offices. One reason for the popularity of Latin American telenovelas is Africa's economic divide. Everybody aspires to be rich and to move into the middle class. These types of stories resonate with people avidly watching the lifestyle they long for.

partly thanks to the educational HIV campaigns that at the time were broadcast intensively by radio in the most affected areas. Freeplay is currently still a respected producer of sustainable radio equipment for development organisations.

Television and mass media The medium made its introduction in the early 20th century. In different parts of the world, scientists worked on the technological development that followed two lines: mechanical and electronic. Initially, you could think of the design as a neutral conduit, which, like many other new products, is neither good nor bad; it depends on how you are going to use it. Television is a very special example, because it has proved to be a huge driver of major cultural changes, becoming a bridge that connects cultures through images and stories. Values and ideologies are transferred via television. Politicians and strict religious leaders have understood this all too well, which explains why television is also seen as a threat to traditional values. Especially for older generations who are not used to media that is free of time and place via the Internet, television is an important part of a daily ritual. The stories and role models represented regulate our social need for connectedness and identity at home, but especially beyond. Television expands our thinking on an infinite number of topics. It also makes it possible to learn about other cultures and global changes. The negative side, however, is that dominant stories and role models often misrepresent reality. The nuances and values of minorities are underexposed, and this is at the expense of diversity and minorities' own identity. Meanwhile, the range of stories has become so diverse, due to the technical possibilities, that you might wonder whether and how individuals are able to find their way and to sustain their own value systems. If only it were possible. In some countries with little money for education and media development, for example, people depend on programmes broadcast on state television and aimed at dominant cultures. If there is no budget or education for minorities to create their own programmes, chances are that their values will not be represented. This example illustrates once again that looking with a cultural lens at products goes much further than the ease of use of a remote control or the desirable appearance of a flat screen.

In the 1950s, film actors like James Dean wore T-shirts onscreen, making them a symbol of rebellion. The fashion label 'Clan de Banlieue' refers to the French name for low-income sub-urban housing projects where immigrants reside, turning a negative connotation into a badge of honour. The Punks had their own codes of shock and awe, like this Vivian Westwood T-shirt.

T-shirt The T-shirt is the most popular piece of clothing worldwide, adopted by almost every culture or subculture, and used for every conceivable purpose. However, the origin of the T-shirt is not entirely clear. It is said that British soldiers wore the garment under their military uniforms during World War I. Others say that French soldiers may have worn it even earlier. It is even considered to date back to the late 19th century, when labourers would cut their long one-piece underwear in half to keep cool in warmer months of the year.

In 1920, the writer F. Scott Fitzgerald first coined the name T-shirt in his novel 'This Side of Paradise', describing the set of clothing the protagonist took with him on his trip to New England. In the same year, the name found its way into the Merriam-Webster dictionary.

However, the first T-shirt was manufactured as such in the period between the Mexican-American War in 1898 and 1913, when the American navy used them as standard undershirts, and other branches of the military followed suit. It was their popularity among the armed forces that allowed the T-shirt to switch from being just an item of uniform underwear to becoming an everyday clothing staple. By the late 1950s, the T-shirt had seeped into American pop culture, sported by Hollywood icons like James Dean and Marlon Brando. Through their rebellious act of wearing something that had first been considered underwear, the T-shirt was transformed from an item of underclothing into famous outerwear. Later, influenced by new industrial production processes for printing and stitching, designers and entrepreneurs discovered the possibility of printing characters (persons and symbols, and from movies and cartoons) onto the fabric. In the 1970s, the T-shirt began to be used as a platform to make powerful statements, such as political statements during the Vietnam War, while Rock and Punk bands and activist groups used it to challenge the general public. Finally, the fashion industry took over, making fashion statements and using the T-shirt for branding. Whether mass-produced or as a single piece, extraordinarily expensive or unbelievably cheap, as a disposable product or a sustainable and durable one, the T-shirt conquered the whole world, and became an integral part of our lives.

Umbrella The basic design is probably more than 4000 years old. Its origin lies in sunny regions such as Egypt, Persia, Greece, and China, where the umbrella provided shade against a searing sun. The name refers to *umbra* being the Latin word for 'shad-

High-class English gentlemen had their own particular strict dress code: black, pinstripe, bowler hat, and umbrella. For his intricately engineered physical comedy, film maker and actor Buster Keaton played with the common relationships we have with our functional accessories, such as the umbrella, while Hong Kong protesters turned its protective function into a symbol of rebellion.

ow'. Or the French *parasol*, with *para* meaning 'to stop' or 'to shield' and *sol* meaning 'sun'. The water-resistant version, designed in China, made the design relevant in Northern Europe with its rainy climates. Initially, it was still an item typically for use by women, but when the famous writer and traveller through Persia, John Hanway (1712-1786), started using the umbrella publicly, it also became popular among men, although preferably folded when not in use and held like a walking stick.

The first umbrellas were made of wood and whalebone, with an alpaca or oiled canvas canopy. The curved handle was of hardwood and was made by hand. In 1852, during the industrial revolution, the steel maker Samuel Fox developed the steel-ribbed version. (The steel was also used as boning for corsets, a women's undergarment in vogue at the time). In 1928, the Viennese student of sculpture, Slava Horowitz, designed a collapsible variant of the umbrella. Austrian companies put it into production and the German company Knips followed, which explains the common name in Germany for a 'folding umbrella': the 'knips'.

The umbrella has now become a product used and sold globally, but with a localy varying usage and symbolic meaning. Since 2014, the umbrella is the symbol for a protest movement in Hong Kong that aims to protect democracy in Hong Kong; the Umbrella Movement. This name arose from the use of umbrellas as a defense against the Hong Kong Police's use of pepper spray to disperse the crowds.

Toy bricks Lego represents a collection of colourful plastic interlocking bricks accompanied by a series of mini-figures and a variety of specific building elements. In 1949, Ole Kirk Christiansen (1891-1958) started, among other new products, an early version of what we now call Lego in his wooden toy business. The company name was derived from the Danish 'LEg GOdt', which means 'play well'. The small plastic bricks were based on the Kiddicraft Self-Locking Bricks, which were patented in the United Kingdom in 1939 and released in 1947. Lego had received a sample from a supplier of injection moulding machines. The bricks, originally made from cellulose acetate, were developed on the basis of the traditional stackable wooden blocks popular at the time. The popularity of Lego is due to the value that Christiansen advocated

Lego offers the possibility of building whatever you want and can imagine. 'The treachery of images' by Belgian surrealist painter René Magritte is an image of a pipe with the text 'This is not a pipe'. It reveals that humans can only deal with reality by describing it indirectly, by using signs or language. 'Is it not a pipe?' Margritte was once asked. 'Try filling it with tabacco', he replied.

A common idea in Western countries is that Japan deviously or ingenuously copied others' designs. The notion ignores Japan's history of creative exchanges with the outside world, and the particular myths, philosophies, and concepts that are emblematic of the origins and originality of copying in Japan. Japanese design stands open to all ideas and influences, selecting the best and improving on them.

and passed on to his son and employees under the motto 'det bedste er ikke for godt': 'only the best is good enough'. Lego is a great example of how a product, based on a universal idea of what playing and creating is, can simultaneously adapt to a specific culture. In the 1970s, Lego started to introduce themes such as town, castle, and space, and later followed with many more, including action heroes and themes, such as the Paralympics in Rio. The colourful bricks are used as educational material by children in schools, and even by adults in companies to develop visions and creative solutions. Over the decades, thanks to its open and modular form, Lego has been able to adapt constantly to changes, including the most recent technological developments such as robotics and digitisation.

Pointer booklets are designed to bridge the language barriers that travellers encounter in unfamiliar places. Initially, such booklets seem to be a simple, ingenious, and effective solution. Until you discover that every image is culturally charged and that images – like colours and sounds – do not mean the same thing everywhere. Moreover, showing luxurious product images to people who cannot afford them can be experienced as provocative and offensive.

The Walkman Music is considered the most universal and enigmatic of all human cultural expression. An abstract universal language that is at least 40,000 years old, it has been used both to accompany rituals and to be played for its own sake. It is difficult to define music, since it only exists in the moment of its being played and heard. That changed in 1877, however, when Thomas Jefferson Edison invented the phonograph, which could capture and replay any music.

Prior to this, and dating back to 1400 BC, the only way to register music was in very limited forms of melodic notation. In 1252, Safi al-Din al-Urmawi developed a new form of musical notation that included the representation of rhythm. The Catholic Church's intention of achieving ecclesiastical uniformity in mediaeval Europe marked a next phase in the development of modern music notation, and it continued to develop as new musical instrument technologies were developed. But

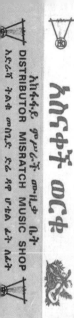

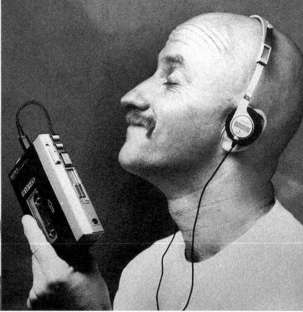

'Cassette culture' has become a widely used, appropriate way of describing the variety of social practices generated by audiocassette hardware. Next to recording music, cassettes are also used as audio letters for labourers or people displaced to war zones. An audio letter can be replayed among relatives as a surrogate for the physical form of the absent relative.

In the 1970s, cheap blank tapes drove the creation of musical undergrounds. From mix tapes, passed around by bands eager to become known, to Grandmaster Flash's $1 per minute customised hip-hop party tapes. By the early 1980s, a recognisable international home tapers' underground network existed that had discovered the cassette as a reusable medium, similar to scratch paper for making quick notes.

it was the invention of the phonograph that marked the most drastic revolution, and to an extent that has permanently changed its nature and character. From the moment that any musical performance could be captured in a recording, it became a commodity that could be reproduced and sold. From being creators, musicians were transformed into suppliers for a new industry that used their recordings to sell phonographs and radios. It was a big business that later developed into the even bigger mass media and entertainment industry.

This worldwide revolution has paved the way for numerous new technologies involved in capturing and distributing music. One was the magnetophon steel tape recorder, another milestone that drastically improved sound quality. In 1963, the Dutch electronics company Philips further developed magnetic tape recordings into a cassette technology for portable speech-only dictation machines. Once the poor recording quality began to improve, youngsters embraced these small cassette recorders as an affordable alternative to the large reel-to-reel music recorders, which enabled them to assemble personal play lists from radio broadcasts or vinyl records. This development triggered an unforeseen revolution in African countries, where local musicians discovered new distribution possibilities and low production costs based on the cheap and accessible cassette technology. Independent releases of local artists and music genres flourished, generating a boost in sales of simple transistor cassette players, a change that no outsider could have imagined.

In the late 1960s, pre-recorded cassette tapes began to make listening to music mobile with the introduction of cassette players integrated in car radios. Portable stereo cassette decks where designed for listening to music together wherever you wanted, like the boom boxes made popular by the early hip hop community in the 1980s in New York.

The story goes that Sony founder and designer Masaru Ibuka liked to listen to classical music when travelling by plane or train. He did not want to bother fellow passengers, however, which aligns with an important value in Japanese culture. This led to the revolutionary design of the first hand-size portable music player with headphones, introduced in 1979 as the Sony Walkman. Since that moment, listening

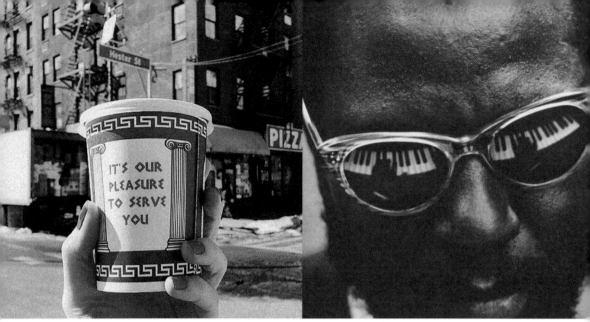

Classics from the New York cultural melting pot: The iconic Anthora coffee cup, designed to appeal to the city's Greek restaurant owners, has become an enduring symbol of New York City. New York jazz pianist, High Priest of BeBop Thelonious Monk was renowned for his distinct self-styled look, which included remarkable suits, hats, and sunglasses.

to music of one's choice while en route somewhere is a matter of course. Being able to customise a playlist combined with the privacy of listening through headphones launched a revolution in portable electronics that instantly became an international success. It paved the way for next generations of micro electronic devices such as iPods, and then for smartphones that are becoming even lighter, faster, smaller, and advanced as well as more integrated personal extensions of the owner.

Anthora coffee cup A stereotypical example notable as a cultural symbol is the Anthora, a paper coffee cup designed in 1963 by Leslie Buck. Born in what was then Czechoslovakia, Buck had survived World War II, after which he and his brother travelled emigrated to New York, where they started a paper cup company, the Sherri Cup Co. Designed to appeal to Greek-owned coffee shops, widely represented in New York City at that time, the Anthora cup featured an image of an amphora and the colours of the Greek flag together with the words 'we are happy to serve you' in an angular typeface resembling ancient Greek. With his accented English, Buck would have pronounced amphora as 'anthora', hence the name. Sales of the cup reached 500 million in 1994, and the Anthora has been called 'the most successful cup in history.'

'I don't know where jazz is going. Maybe it's going to hell. You can't make anything go anywhere. It just happens.' (Thelonious Monk)

Sunglasses Already in prehistoric times, Inuit people wore 'glasses' of flattened walrus-tusk ivory with narrow slits to block the sun's harmful reflected rays. In the 12th century, lenses made of flat panes of smoky quartz were used in China, including by judges who used these glasses to disguise their facial expressions while interrogating witnesses. Much later, in the 18th century, the English optician and designer James Ayscough developed glasses with coloured lenses, intended for people who had a visual impairment. At the beginning of the 20th century, celebrities started wearing them to avoid eye contact in public. By 1938, sunglasses were a new fad on the streets in big cities in the US, where 20 million pairs were sold each year, though only about 25 percent were based on doctor's prescriptions. In the 1940s, jazz pianist Thelonious Monk made sunglasses 'cool' by wearing stylish models during concerts inside dark nightclubs.

Greg LeMond won the closest Tour de France in history, completing the 3,219-kilometre race with a victory margin of only eight seconds, thanks to a new Boone Lennon-designed aero bar. The Thor 32, designed by Hurley Electric Laundry Equipment Company, introduced the first automated washing machine in 1907, saving women many hours of hard daily work.

Before the shot clock was introduced in 1954, basketball was struggling to gain traction as a major mainstream sport in America. Scoring was low and, much to the fans' disappointment, teams would often decide to hold the ball and stall once they were in front. Thanks to the clock, the scoring average jumped to 93.

Clap skate The clap skate's design makes it possible to achieve a further push or 'clap' when the skater takes off, which increases speed. The idea of a hinged skate had already been described and patented in 1894 by Karl Hannes in Germany. It was not until 1979, however, that the sports scientist Gerrit Jan van Ingen Schenau in Amsterdam reinvented the clap skate. Apparently, the time was ripe, although the introduction was not easy. The design had to overcome the existing skating culture with its ingrained judgements and traditions. This was difficult, because it also required making an adjustment to the skating technique itself. Professional sports cultures are conservative, and innovations often rely on role models willing to pioneer the new product. For example, Greg Lemond won the Tour de France in 1989 with the introduction of a primitive form of aerodynamic time-trial handlebar. As with the clap skate, people were sceptical and ridiculed the design, but it eventually led to a special time-trial bike with many more technical innovations. Only when multiple victories are achieved do changes proceed rapidly and the innovation becomes the new standard.

Housekeeping For centuries, 'keeping the nest clean' had been the women's domain. In the 19th and early 20th centuries, the lower classes, middle classes, and domestic workers – in Western Europe in particular – spent a great deal of time doing housework. The upper middle class outsourced these chores. Eventually, a steadily growing middle class started copying the upper classes by doing likewise. Early feminists encouraged these developments because they would liberate women, giving them time and opportunities to leave the home, do paid work, and thereby contribute to society in an equal way. From the end of the 19th century, commercial laundries changed rapidly from small, labour-intensive businesses to large-scale capital-intensive factories, equipped with steam engines and modern technology. The Second World War, however, interrupted the trend of laundry being done as an industrial service, resulting in the acceptance of household washing machines, albeit more than 60 years after the initial developments. Influenced by the rising prosperity, a growing middle class, and a culture in which the modern woman slowly began to

The traditional gathering around the table for the family dinner is disappearing. Meanwhile, in big cities, take-away food or delivery meals are on the rise, bringing all sorts of food from food cultures around the world. This rapidly developing new economy is having a big impact on our relationship with food: i.e. what we eat, how we eat, where we eat, and when we eat.

Computer software for food delivery helps consumers to order from online menus, pay online, determine the most efficient routes for carriers, track order and delivery times, and so on. Customers use satellite navigation tracking over the Internet for real-time monitoring of delivery vehicles. The design for packaging and transport containers is a big issue, however, also as regards the environment.

derive her identity from technologically advanced household products, the washing machine, like other household appliances, gained in popularity. In the 50 years that followed, the washing machine conquered the world, during which period its design hardly changed. And though the use of new materials in the fashion industry together with environmental legislation have made the machine 'smarter', it remains a white, noisy, water-hungry rectangular box.

The cultural impact of the washing machine and other household innovations – such as vacuum cleaners, microwaves, and dishwashers – on family life has turned out to be far more dramatic. Along with contraceptives, these machines have probably had the most influence on women's emancipation. Women became more independent when most housekeeping tasks could be transferred to machines, and modern family life became increasingly detached and individualistic.

Kitchen and cooking For centuries, local situations have determined how we grow and process food (literally cultivate); what we eat; how we eat, and with whom, when, where, and in what order. The geographical environment and local conditions have determined our food options, habits, and social norms. As a result of globalisation, next to technological and economic developments, what we eat is now linked increasingly less to place and time. Food cultures meet and change, including the significance of the kitchen and its appliances. From separated spaces in which women played a central role, kitchens were transformed into a social space where family rituals provided coherence in relationships and enhanced social values. The introduction of the microwave and dishwasher removed the need to eat together at a fixed time. Microwave meals made their appearance, and sitting in front of the television with a plate on one's lap replaced sitting together for a meal around the table.

In high economic societies, cooking is no longer a basic need but a way of expressing oneself. The kitchen has become a status symbol, hyped through marketing that promotes professional kitchen islands and tools and gadgets to the consumer market, and through cooking shows that flourish on television and the Internet. In high-density megacities, where people live in very small spaces and food services are cheap

From 1630 onwards, plague docters wore protective clothing and special masks, which were believed to be sufficiently protective. As our global metropolises become ever more congested and polluted, in addition to raincoats and helmets, face masks may become a regular part of our outdoor protective wear, with new cultural features inevitably being added.

and widely available, the kitchen may even be non-existent or reduced to being only a shelf or counter large enough for a microwave. There are, however, still many people living in rural areas, who cook with a stove and spend a substantial part of the day collecting wood. There is a need for solutions that allow more efficient combustion with emissions that are less toxic. Outsiders have designed many alternatives, but implementation is difficult. The dependence on local resources and situations requires designs that cater to the existing local conditions and food culture.

The Venice carnival is famous for its amazing masks, although the original reason for wearing these face coverings remains unknown. Some argue that covering the face in public was a response to Venice's rigid class hierarchies. During Carnival, sumptuary laws were suspended, and people could dress as they liked, avoiding the rules set down in law for professions and social classes. There have been several periods when wearing masks in Venice was prohibited.

Masks The French word *masque* means 'covering to hide or guard the face'; the Catalan *mascarar* means 'blackening the face'; the Mediaeval Latin *masca* refers to 'nightmare'. Either way, a mask has many manifestations and meanings in different cultures. And its functions are many: to punish; to hide or enhance one's identity; to change identity or even to help a person cross between the worlds of the living and the dead; to protect against poisonous gases in a fire or in war situations; to protect against bee stings; and — as used currently by doctors and personnel in hospitals — to protect against viruses. The mask was used to effect by 'plague masters' or 'plague doctors', whose task was to isolate and treat plague victims. To protect themselves, the doctors wore protective clothing and the famous mask with its beak-like nose also filled with herbs and spices to purify the air and to block the stench of illness and death. The long nose unintentionally also helped maintain an added distance from infectious patients. But the mask's main effect was that it frightened people into keeping their distance from the masked doctor, who symbolised the feared and deadly disease. Today people wearing face masks in public often carry the same stigma.

Because of heavily polluted metropolises and experiences with rapidly spreading viruses, for Chinese people it is normal and socially acceptable to wear a face mask in public. In Japan, successive events — including a massive influenza pandemic in which millions of people died, a volcanic eruption, and rapidly increasing industrialisation in the 20th century — forced the population to cover their face with scarves, veils, and masks as a protective measure. The reason for this easy acceptance might

Try to find the thirteenth floor. It is a quirk based on superstition and marketing savvy, as not many tenants seem willing to rent on the thirteenth floor. Beware the Ides of March: the 15th, known as the day in 44 BC when Julius Caesar was murdered. A long list of political tragedies on the same date followed: most recently, the war in Syria in 2011.

During the 2020 Covid-19 pandemic, the USA Centers for Disease Control and Prevention guidelines that suggested Americans should use T-shirts, scarves, handkerchiefs or any other spare fabric to make homemade masks to wear when going to a grocery store. But not realising that this could lead ultimately to a life-or-death situation. For a black man in America, the fear of being mistaken and shot for being an armed robber or assailant was greater than the fear of contracting Covid-19.[12]

also be cultural. In Taoism, breathing is seen as a central element of good health. In addition, many Asian countries have a strongly collectivist culture, where people are careful not to bother others, and serving the collective is an important value. Wearing a mask has the connotation of being mindful of others. Unfortunately, woven-fabric non-surgical masks offer minimal protection against both environmental pollution and viruses; not only can viruses spread in public spaces but they also enter homes where masks are not worn. However, the prophylactic usefulness of the masks is, in a sense, secondary to the more symbolic protection, and therefore they are likely to become more common in the future — including among non-Asians.

Paraskevidekatriaphobia is the scientific name for the irrational fear that people have of Friday the 13th. Several myths explain this fear: for example, the Norse myth about a dinner for twelve gods and a 13th who was not invited, which led to tragedy. In the Middle Ages, the story was told of Jesus having his last supper on Friday with his twelve disciples, a total of 13 persons; next day he was crucified. In Spanish-speaking countries, the unfortunate day falls on Tuesday the 13th, and in Italy it is on Friday the 17th, whereas the 13th is considered a lucky day. In Chinese and Japanese, number 4 is a homonym for the word 'death'. As a result, most Asian companies avoid using these numbers entirely. This kind of widespread superstition has led to hotels and airlines in the US not giving the number 13 to rooms or to seats, respectively, and racing cyclists who are assigned the number 13 try to ward off punctures and crashes by pinning the number upside down on the back of their shirts. The number 39 is known *as the curse of 39* in Afghan culture. Superstitions also abound in events, objects, combinations of colours, and gestures. Spilling salt brings bad luck, while throwing a pinch of salt over your left shoulder reverses it. In Latin America, getting married on a Tuesday should be avoided. In Egypt, opening and closing a pair of scissors without cutting anything ensures something bad will happen. Fortunately, lucky numbers and symbols also exist, such as 7 in the Christian culture. When pronounced, the number 8 in China sounds like

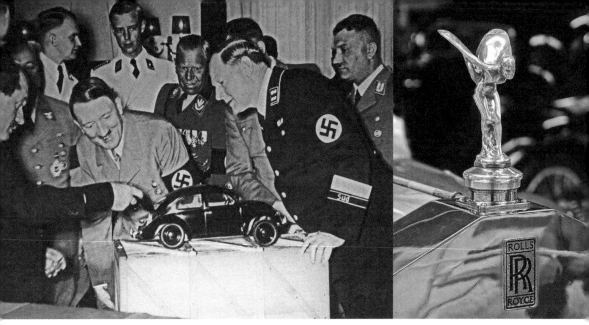

Car designer Ferdinand Porsche presents a scale model of his design for the Volkswagen (literally 'people's car') to Adolf Hitler.
The Spirit of Ecstasy, designed by sculptor Charles Robinson Sykes in 1906, is the ornamental metal sculpture on the bonnet of
Rolls-Royce cars, the most expensive and prestigious automobile designed for the lucky few.

the Chinese word for 'fortune', while good luck is symbolised by white elephants
in Thailand and by four-leaf clovers everywhere. These and other superstitions
shine an illuminating light on our behaviour and learned thinking, illustrating how
symbols and events can mean nothing to one group while being hugely significant
to another.

The cost of a
Volkswagen was
to be no more than
990 Reichsmarks,
and the car was to
have a top speed of
100 KPH and space
for two adults and
one child or three
soldiers and one
machine gun.

Automobility The first cars were either steam powered or had electric or petrol combustion engines. Combustion engines became the standard because there was no electric
infrastructure in rural areas, whereas an infrastructure of petrol stations fuelled by a
powerful Texan oil industry had been rolled out. Thanks to Ford's efficient industrial
production, the Ford Model T, produced between 1908 and 1927, was the first car to
become affordable for consumers in the growing American middle class. It was also the
first car to be produced and assembled in various countries around the world.

It is not without reason that the design and development of the Volkswagen (which
literally means 'people's car') in the 1930s was one of the most important symbols of
Nazi ideology. Adolf Hitler commissioned Ferdinand Porsche to design a car that every
German civilian could own. Because of the Nazis even greater military ambitions,
however, production turned to military vehicles. It was British Army officer Major Ivan
Hirst who restarted the Volkswagen production lines in Wolfsburg in 1945 in order to
hand them over to one of the big international auto companies, including Ford. But none
saw any future for what they called that 'ugly and noisy car', which is why the factory
was turned into a symbol of West German economic regeneration under its car model
name Volkswagen. This decision appeared to be a brilliant move, as the robust and
affordable Volkswagen Beetle turned out to be the most-produced, single make of car
ever. Up until the last production line in Mexico closed in July 2003, 21,529,464 Beetles
had been produced. Its success includes its remarkable revival in the 1960s when the
hippie movement fell in love with its friendly bug shape. It soon became a symbol of
peace and freedom, a symbol that was shared with the extremely successful car with
animal features: the Citroen Ugly Duckling.

Women have been important to the success of the Vespa, as demonstrated by Italian actress and fashion model Elsa Martinelli on the filmset riding a Vespa. The iconic Vespa scooter is produced in thirteen countries and sold around the world, leading to customised versions in Indonesia during an annual festival in Kediri East Java,. And La Dolce Vita Africaine in Mali.

Within 50 years after the introduction of the Ford model, the automobile had conquered the whole world, and has by now almost completely displaced horses, donkeys, camels, and other animals as a means of transport. Car usage varies around the world, but has had a profound impact on all cultures and interconnections. The automobile quickly developed from being a means of transportation to becoming a personal status symbol, with models that looked like spaceships, and with luxury brands that were intended to be affordable only for the lucky few. The car became the most important carrier of cultural symbolism worldwide, representing a culture of its own.

In densely populated areas, individual car ownership already appears to be losing status. The days of the energy-inefficient and polluting combustion-engine cars are numbered, as electric cars are taking over at a speed that until recently was considered impossible. The online service economy is leading young generations to find other ways to travel and to express their identity, giving rise to the question as to how the cultural significance of cars will evolve or give way to a new and as yet unknown culture of mobility.

The wasp The Italian Vespa scooter has been successful for more than 75 years, with a design that has become today's popular standard as an electric means of transport in urban areas. Its story began in Genoa after World War II, when roads in Italy were in poor condition, few people could afford a car, and the post-war industry had to develop a new product for an emerging market. Aviation designer Corradino D'Ascanio, who assisted Enrico Piaggio in designing the Vespa (named after its wasp shape), found existing motorcycles to be bulky, difficult to repair, and dirty. Inspired by the small olive-coloured Cushman Airborne motorcycles dropped by the Americans during World War II, they decided to go for a completely new and user-friendly shape. They moved the gear lever to the steering wheel, and applied a wheel suspension used on airplanes to make changing tires easy. The seating position was designed to provide both safety and comfort. Furthermore, technical and moving parts were hidden behind panels to keep clothing clean. The most iconic part is the low entry-level frame that also made the Vespa attractive for women, who at that time predominantly wore dress-

The Paralympics began as a small gathering of British World War II veterans in 1948, and have become one the largest international sporting events. The event showcases designs to aid athletes and enhance their performance. These innovations have had a profound effect on development aids in everyday life, such as the SuitX exoskeleton.

es and skirts. The Vespa became a cultural icon representing an Italian way of life, popularised by its appearance in films like 'La Dolce Vita', or 'Roman Holiday', with movie stars like Audrey Hepburn and Gregory Peck riding on a Vespa through the sunny Italian streets. The scooter became popular in Asia as a cheap and reliable commuter, with licensed local production lines across Asia.

Wheelchairs and tricycles In a sense, disabled people represent their own culture by way of their circumstances. They often literally cannot move or manage in an environment not designed to include them. In public spaces as well as in private areas, stairs, escalators, lifts, doorways, cars, planes, and chairs constitute physical and social barriers. Aid products that do not fall within the codes or standards of the majority may unintentionally encourage stigmatisation and social exclusion, which often applies to several minority groups within a local dominant culture. Products designed to accommodate a disability only become accepted when one minority outnumbers the others: eyeglasses, for example, that once only served the primary function of improving vision for people with a visual disability have now become a fashion item used to express one's status and personality. Walking sticks and walkers are so common these days that they are taken into account in design briefs for public entrances and elevators. For wheelchairs and tricycles it may still be different, as these users remain minorities.

Windmills and watermills Medieval Europe changed radically thanks to the mill. Windmills and watermills replaced human labour, the first industrial revolution started. According to historiography, this technical ingenuity was invented in China and Persia (present-day Iran) at the beginning of our Christian era, but - like many other innovations - did not become successful until centuries later in evolved variants. Most windmills, as we still know them today, have a horizontal axis that can be turned to the wind. In the 18th century, depending on the landscape and climate, wind or water mill became extremely popular and used for various purposes, including grinding grains, pumping water for land and salt extraction,

A Dutch windmill, detail from a painting by Jacob Isaacksz van Ruisdael in 1628, and a modern offshore wind farm for the production of electricity. Onshore wind farms have been criticised as being a blemish on the landscape. One may wonder whether people in the past had the same objections. In the 19th century, before steam engines took over, the Netherlands had 10,000 windmills.

The microclimate generated by wind turbines on land improves crops, as it prevents the late spring and early autumn frosts, and also reduces the action of pathogenic fungi that grow on the leaves. Even at the height of summer heat, the lowering of 2.5-3 degrees above the crops due to turbulence can improve the cultivation of corn.

peeling rice, pressing olives and rapeseed, and processing cocoa, mustard, pepper, tobacco, paper and sawing wood. What is striking is the enormous diversity in techniques and shapes, which was emphasized even more by giving the mills their own name, just like with ships. The significance of a mill went beyond industrial utility usage; it also contributed to the user's identity. The introduction of the oil and coal-fired steam engine has driven the mill out, but due to the oil crisis in the 1970s and increasing environmental problems, the windmill has risen from its ashes, albeit in a new form. It is remarkable now that the wind turbines (a new name for a new form and function) are very similar and stand together in a kind of anonymous group like gulls or geese together, without an owner.

Colour as a cultural code The significance and effect of colour in design depends strongly on the application, but remains abstract in most cultures. China has a different and more powerful scale of colour symbolism, with black, red, qing (a fusion of the idea of green and blue), white, and yellow defined as standard colours related to the five main elements: metal, fire, water, wood, and air. Black is linked to water. The Chinese word for black is 'hei' which stands for bad luck, irregularity, and illegality. Black should not be worn to auspicious occasions like weddings, and a person's portrait is placed in a black frame only if the person is deceased. Yet black is widely used for fancy consumer goods such as watches and electronics. White represents the element of metal, and symbolises purity and innocence. In some instances, it is associated with death, since it is the colour worn at funerals. The colour red represents fire and brings good luck, which is why Chinese brides wear red dresses, gifts are wrapped in red, and red is the dominant colour in Chinese New Year celebrations. A name should never be written in red, however, because in earlier times the names of those sentenced to death were written in chicken blood. Yellow represents earth, and is an imperial colour depicting power, royalty, and prosperity. Nowadays, however, the colour yellow denotes pornography in publications in China, so be careful when using yellow in print. Blue represents the wood element and also symbolises spring, immortality, and advancement. Green

In the 1860s, the US government started issuing paper money called greenbacks. They were printed with green ink as a measure to prevent counterfeiting. In 1929, the government reduced the size of all paper currency to cut down on manufacturing costs. The small-sized bills continued to be printed with green ink, however, because the ink was plentiful and durable, and the colour green was associated with stability.

stands for wealth, harmony, growth, cleanliness, and freedom from contamination, but is not associated with being environment friendly. Purple stands for divinity and immortality. In modern times, it is used to represent love or romance.

In many cultures, depending on the context of use, red, for instance, may be the colour of love but also of danger. Black is often used to express both mourning and importance (black limousines), whereas other cultures use white for these purposes. In politics, blue often represents conservatism and liberalism, while red stands for communism or socialism. Green obviously is the colour for environmentalists. However, the application of any colour will never be judged or interpreted more intently than by the Chinese.

It costs about 5 cents to produce a $1 bill and around 13 cents to make a $100 bill, the highest denomination in circulation. The estimated life span of a $1 bill is close to 6 years; for a $100 bill it's 15 years, and for a $50 bill it's 3.7 years.

Money This phenomenon is a decisive factor for all cultures worldwide. In its most basic form, it is a medium of exchange to facilitate trade, and the manifestation of this concept began in very early times with 'currency' that included rare metals, stones, and shells. Meanwhile, it has become coins, banknotes, and securities associated with our contemporary digital transactions via online payments, apps, virtual coins, and algorithms, all speeding up lightning-fast financial transactions around the globe. In essence, money is nothing but an agreement based on a general belief in its existence. Even the determination of value is based completely on a level of belief and trust, while at the same time it has become the absolute measure of all things. One might think that only people who do not know what they want are in pursuit of the possession of money, because money bears the promise of everything imaginable. Even our most valuable works of art, which represent our deepest shared cultural values, have been reduced both to negotiable investments and cultural signifiers for privileged individuals.

How this object of desire has been able to hijack the imagination of the whole world remains a mystery. The result is a curious ideology involving a culture that revolves around the acquisition of private property and the pursuit of profit maximisation. This desire for money has reached the masses, and leads mainly

Early assumptions held that Cargo Cult practitioners simply did not understand technology, colonisation, distribution systems, or capitalist economics. The ritual was seen as an attempt to acquire goods after trade had been interrupted. However, many of its practitioners focused on maintaining and creating new social relationships, with material relationships serving that purpose.

to undesirable fringe phenomena such as human exploitation and environmental damage. The fact that, for no apparent reason, all the ingredients for our daily nutrition travel across the globe is not the inescapable course of things — it is a situation we created ourselves. As Slovenian philosopher and cultural critic Slavoj Zizek said about our tendency to accept all of this as normal: 'It is easier to imagine the end of the world than the end of capitalism'.

Cargo Cults have vanished in the southwest Pacific. What remains is a wild tangle of popular Cargoist discourse. It continues to be a confusing ethnographic reality that cannot be claimed to exist in the minds of Western observers alone. Melanesians meanwhile use the term as an insult when outraged by the ludicrous plans or claims made by political rivals.

Cargo Cult An American base that was built in the Pacific on the island of Melanesia shortly after World War II introduced Western luxury goods to the local residents. As they did not understand where all the cargo that was brought in by airplanes came from, or where and how the items were made, they attributed the origin of the goods to deceased ancestors over whom the outsiders had taken control. The arrival of these luxury goods was considered to be the dawning of a new era in which justice and prosperity would rule. To rectify this seizure of power over the goods from their ancestors, the islanders began to imitate the behaviour of the newcomers, but with no knowledge about the meaning or purpose of the military activities they witnessed, such as marching, drills, making inventory lists, and so on. With rifles, uniforms, insignia, writing utensils, drawers, radios, and even an airplane made of coconuts and straw, they copied the activities of Western military personnel as rituals for the purpose of attracting cargo.

This complex phenomenon seems related to Millenarianism in many other cultures. It represents a belief in a fundamental change or a revolution in society following a catastrophe or a dramatic experience, after which everything will finally work out. These cults often develop in a crisis or social stress situation under the leadership of a charismatic figure who has had a vision or a mystical dream of the future. It is usually a synthesis of traditional and foreign elements, often linked to an old order that needs to be restored.

The only way to be able to look at our own culture objectively is through the eyes of the other. In the final example, it is not only the outsider or minority who is investigated as a curious phenomenon but also the dominant global culture of consumerism, with its material fetishism that is presented in a mirror image.

References and Further Reading Many books, papers and other scientific sources have been consulted and referred to in the text. Further reading will give you a better understanding and will do justice to the authors work, how their theories and methods should be understood.

- Ahmad, J., Goldar, B. & Misra, S. (2006). Rural communities' preferences for arsenic mitigation options in Bangladesh. *Journal of Water and Health*, 4 (4), 463–477.
- Appadurai, A. (Ed.) (1988). *The Social Life of Things. Commodities in Cultural Perspective*. Cambridge: Cambridge University Press.
- Baird, T. D., & Hartter, J. (2017). Livelihood diversification, mobile phones and information diversity in Northern Tanzania. *Land Use Policy*, 67, 460-471.
- Banks, J.A. (1998). The Lives and Values of Researchers: Implications for Educating Citizens in a Multicultural Society. *Educational Researcher*, 27(7), 4-17.
- Barthes, R. (1957). *Mythologies*. Paris: Editions du Seuil.
- Basu, T. (2018). *Who is Krampus? Explaining the horrific Christmas beast*. National Geographic. Retrieved at April 2020 from https://www.nationalgeographic.com/news/2018/12/131217-krampus-christmas-santa-devil/.
- Bates, D.G. & Plog, F. (1976). *Cultural Anthropology* (3rd ed.). New York: McGraw-Hill.
- Bell, G. (2001). Looking across the Atlantic: Using ethnographic methods to make sense of Europe. *Intel Technology Journal*, 2001 (3).
- Bennett, M.J. (2004). *Becoming interculturally competent*. In J.S. Wurzel (Ed.) Toward multiculturalism: A reader in multicultural education. Newton, MA: Intercultural Resource Corporation.
- Berry, J.W. (2005). Acculturation: Living successfully in two cultures. *International Journal of Intercultural Relations*, 29(2005), 697–712.
- Bezhan, F. (2012). The Deadly Consequences Of Cultural Insensitivity In Afghanistan. Radio Free Europe. Retrieved at April 2020 from https://www.rferl.org/a/afghanistan-deadly-consequences-of-cultural-insensitiviy/24707511.html.
- Boradkar, P. (2010). *Designing things: A critical introduction to the culture of objects*. Oxford: Berg.
- Brinkmann, U. & van Weerdenburg, O. (2014). *Intercultural Readiness: Four competences for working across cultures*. London: Palgrave Macmillan.
- Briscoe, S. (2005). *The Ultimate Sashiko Sourcebook: Patterns, Projects, and Inspirations*. Wisconsin: Davi and Charles Brunel House.
- Campbell, C. (2019). *How China Is Using "Social Credit Scores" to Reward and Punish Its Citizens*. Time. Retrieved at April 2020 from https://time.com/collection/davos-2019/5502592/china-social-credit-score/.
- Cieraad, I. (2002). Out of my kitchen! Architecture, gender, and domestic efficiency. *The Journal of Architecture*, 7(3), 263-279.
- Clarke, A.J. (ed.) (2018). *Design Anthropology - Object cultures in transition*. London: Bloomsbury Academic.
- de Jongh, E. (2019). *The Malleable Rembrandt: How Dutch art is used in debates about identity*. The low countries. Retrieved at April 2020 from https://www.the-low-countries.com/article/malleable-rembrandt.

- de Mooij, M.K. (2004). *Consumer behaviour and culture: Consequences for global marketing and advertising*. London: Sage Publications.
- de Rijk, T.R.A. (2010). *Norm=Form*. Deventer: Thieme Art BV.
- de Rijk, T.R.A. (2014). On Design, Culture and the Future. Inaugural lecture for Delft University of Technology and Leiden University, p.11. Retrieved December 2014, from http://issuu.com/whatdesigncando/docs/wdcd_2014_book_timo.
- du Gay, P. (1997). *Production of culture/cultures of production*. London: Sage in association with the Open University.
- du Gay, P., Hall, S., Janes, L., Mackay, H. & Negus, K. (1997). *Doing Cultural Studies: The story of the Sony Walkman*. London: Sage Publications, p.59.
- Elias, N. (1978). *The Civilizing Process, Vol 1 The History of Manners*. Oxford: Basil Blackwell.
- Ende, L. van den (2016). *The Power of Rituals - A Study of Transition Rituals in the Life Cycle of Complex Construction Projects*. Doctoral Thesis faculty of Social Sciences VU Amsterdam.
- Engeström, Y. (2001). Expansive learning at work: Toward an activity theoretical reconceptualization. *Journal of Education and Work*, 14(1), 133–156.
- Evancie, A. (2013). The Surprising Sartorial Culture Of Congolese 'Sapeurs'. NPR Picture Show. Retrieved at Arpil 2020 from https://www.npr.org/sections/picture-show/2013/05/07/181704510/the-surprising-sartorial-culture-of-congolese-sapeurs?t=1584871395728&t=1586766231664.
- Gaver, B., Dunne, T., & Pacenti, E. (1999). Design: Cultural probes. *Interactions*, 6(1), 21-29.
- Geertz, C. (1973). *The interpretation of cultures*. New York: Harper Torchbooks (5043).
- Giaccardi, E., Cila, N., Speed, C., & Caldwell, M. (2016). *Thing Ethnography: Doing Design Research with Non-humans*. In proceedings of Designing of Interactive Systems 2016 (pp. 377–387). New York: ACM Press.
- Gorrie, N. (2017). *Chanel needs to understand Indigenous anger. There's nothing 'luxury' about it*. The Guardian. Retrieved at Arpil 2020 from https://www.theguardian.com/commentisfree/2017/may/17/chanel-needs-to-understand-indigenous-anger-theres-nothing-luxury-about-it.
- Hall, E.T. (1973). *The silent language*. New York: Anchor books.
- Hall, E.T. (1976). *Beyond Culture*. New York: Anchor Books.
- Hao, C. (2019). *Cultura - Achieving intercultural empathy through contextual user research in design*. Doctoral Thesis, Delft University of Technology, Delft.
- Hao, C., van Boeijen, A.G.C., Stappers, P.J. (2017). *Towards Cultura: a communication toolkit for designers to gain empathic insights across cultural boundaries*. In proceedings of IASDR.
- Harari, Y.N. (2012). *Sapiens: A brief history of humankind*. London: Random House.

- Harari, Y.N. (2015). *Homo Deus: A brief history of tomorrow.* London: Random House.
- Harford, T. (2017). *'The devil's rope': How barbed wire changed America.* BBC News. Revtrieved at April 2020 from https://www.bbc.com/news/business-40448594.
- Hart, M.T. (2019). The case for caseless iPhones Fanatics of case-free phones say it's about design, but could it really be about status? Vox. Retrieved April 2020 at https://www.vox.com/the-goods/2019/5/30/18644637/iphone-no-case-caseless-design.
- Harris, T. (2016). *How Technology is Hijacking Your Mind — from a Magician and Google Design Ethicist.* Thrive Global. Retrieved at April 2020 from https://medium.com/thrive-global/how-technology-hijacks-peoples-minds-from-a-magician-and-google-s-design-ethicist-56d62ef5edf3.
- Hellemans, B.S. (2014). *Cultuur* (from the series 'Elementaire deeltjes'). Amsterdam: AUP.
- History.com Editors (n.d.). *Day of the Dead (Día de los Muertos).* HISTORY. Retrieved at April 2020 from https://www.history.com/topics/halloween/day-of-the-dead.
- Hofstede, G.H., & Hofstede, G.J. (2005). *Cultures and organizations, software of the mind* (2nd ed.). New York: McGraw-Hill.
- Hofstede, G.H., Hofstede, G.J., & Minkov, M. (2010). *Cultures and organizations, software of the mind* (3rd ed.). New York: McGraw-Hill USA.
- Honold, P. (2000). Culture and context: An empirical study for the development of a framework for the elicitation of cultural influence in product use. *International Journal of Human-Computer Interaction, 12*(4), 327-345.
- House, R.J., Hanges, P.J., Javidan, M., Dorfman, P.W. & Gupta, V. (2004). *Culture, leadership and organizations: The GLOBE study of 62 Societies.* London: Sage Publications Inc.
- Huang, H. (2012). Why Chinese people play Western classical music: Transcultural roots of music philosophy. International Journal of Music Education, 30(2), 161-176.
- IRC-Center (n.d.). *Inter Cultural Readiness Check.* Retrieved from https://www.irc-center.com.
- Johnson, R. (1986). What is Cultural Studies Anyway? *Social Text* (16), 38-80.
- Klein, N., & Sawchuk, K. (2000). No logo: taking aim at the brand bullies. *Canadian Journal of Communication, 25*(4), 576.
- Koops B.J. (2008). *Criteria for normative technology - The acceptability of 'codes as law' in light of democratic and constitutional values.* In: Brownsword, R. and Yeung, K. (eds.), Regulating technologies - Legal futures, regulatory frames and technological fixes. Oxford: Hart, 1974.
- Kroeber, A.L. & Kluckhohn, C. (1952). Culture: A Critical Review of Concepts and Definitions, (Vol. 47). Cambridge, USA: *Peabody Museum of American Archaeology and Ethnology Papers.*
- Kuijer, S.C. (2015). *Implications of Social Practice Theory for Sustainable Design.* Doctoral Thesis. Delft University of Technology, Delft.
- Latour, B. (1992). *Where are the missing masses? Sociology of a few mundane artefacts.* In Bijker, W. and Law, J., Shaping Technology - Building Society. Studies in Sociotechnical Change (pp. 225-259). Cambridge: The MIT Press.
- Leenes, R.E. (2010). *Harde lessen - Apologie van technologie als reguleringsinstrument.* Tilburg: Universiteit van Tilburg.
- Levine, R. (2006). *A geography of time; the temporal misadventures of a social psychologist.* Oxford: Oneworld Publications.
- Lindholm, C., Keinonen, T. & Kiljander, H. (2003). *Mobile Usability: How Nokia Changed the Face of the Mobile Phone.* New York: McGraw-Hill Professional.
- Llewellyn, M. (2004). Designed by women and designing women: gender, planning and the geographic kitchen in Britain 1917-1946. *Cultural geographies, 11*(1), 2-60.
- Loewy, R. (1951). *Never Leave Well Enough Alone.* New York: Simon and Schuster.
- Margolin, V. (2007). Design, the future and the human spirit. *Design Issues, 23*(3).
- Mattelmäki, T. (2006). *Design Probes.* Doctoral Thesis, University of Art and Design Helsinki.
- Meiling, C. (2017). *Dishwasher boom shows appliance is a future 'kitchen star'.* ChinaDaily. Retrieved at Retrieved at April 2020 from https://www.chinadaily.com.cn/business/2017-11/20/content_34754543.htm.
- Menand, L. (2019). *How Cultural Anthropologists Redefined Humanity - A brave band of scholars set out to save us from racism and sexism. What happened?* New Yorker, Retrieved at April 2020 from https://www.newyorker.com/magazine/2019/08/26/how-cultural-anthropologists-redefined-humanity.
- Meyer, E. (2016). *The Culture Map (INTL ED): Decoding How People Think, Lead, and Get Things Done Across Cultures.* Public Affairs.
- Mink, A. (2016). *Design for Well-Being: An Approach for Understanding Users' Lives in Design for Development,* Doctoral Thesis, Faculty of Industrial Design Engineering, Delft University of Technology.
- Mink, A., Hoque, B.A, Khanam, S. & van Halem, D. (2019). Mobile crowd participation to root small-scale piped water supply systems in India and Bangladesh. *Journal of Water, Sanitation and Hygiene for Development, 9* (1), 139-151.
- Nakata, C. & Weidner, K. (2012). Enhancing new product adoption at the base of the pyramid: a contextualized model. *Journal of Product Innovation Management, 29* (1), 21–32.
- Niazi, F., Naseem, M., Khurshid, Z., Zafar, M. S., & Almas, K. (2016). Role of Salvadora persica chewing stick (miswak): A natural toothbrush for holistic oral health. *European journal of dentistry, 10*(02), 301-308.
- Oatman-Stanford, H. (2012). *Hello Sailor! The Nautical Roots of Popular Tattoos.* Collecors Weekly. Retrieved at April 2020 from https://www.collectorsweekly.com/articles/the-nautical-roots-of-the-modern-tattoo/.
- Okakura, K. (2012). *The book of tea.* Jazzybee Verlag.
- Otto, T., & Smith, R.C. (2013). *Design Anthropology: A distinct style of knowing.* In W. Gunn, T. Otto & R.C. Smith, Design anthropology: Theory and Practice. London: Bloomsbury.
- Ozkaramanli, D., Desmet, P.M., & Özcan, E. (2016). Beyond resolving dilemmas: Three design directions for addressing intrapersonal concern conflicts. *Design Issues, 32*(3), 78-91.

- Ozkaramanli, D., Desmet, P.M.A. & Özcan, E. (2017). From teatime cookies to rain-pants: Resolving personal dilemmas through design using three levels of concern conflicts. *International Journal of Design Creativity and Innovation,* 1-16.
- Ozkaramanli, D., Fokkinga, S.F., Desmet, P.M.A., Balkan, E., & George, E. (2013). *Recreating AlaTurca; consumer goal conflicts as a creative driver for innovation.* In D.S. Fellows (Ed.), Brilliant Transformations: Proceedings of Qualitative Research 2013, Valencia, 17-19 November. Amsterdam (NL): ESOMAR.
- Papanek, V. (1971). *Design for the real world – Human Ecology and Social Change.* London: Thames and Hudson.
- Peterson, B. (2004). *Cultural Intelligence.* London: Intercultural Press.
- Popham, P. (2013). *So what is it about Jeff Koons that has so captured art world's imagination as Balloon Dog sells for record $58m?* Independent. Retrieved at April 2020 from https://www.independent.co.uk/arts-entertainment/art/features/so-what-is-it-about-jeff-koons-that-has-so-captured-art-world-s-imagination-as-balloon-dog-sells-for-8943284.html.
- Raijmakers, B. & Miller, S. (2016). *Viewfinders – Thoughts on Visual design research.* London: STBY Ltd.
- Razzaghi, M., Ramirez, M. & Zehner, R. (2009). Cultural patterns in product design ideas: comparison between Australian and Iranian student concepts. *Design Studies,* 30, 438-461.
- Ro, C. (2019). *The peculiar bathroom habits of Westerners.* BBC Future. Retrieved at April 2020 from https://www.bbc.com/future/article/20191004-the-peculiar-bathroom-habits-of-westerners.
- Rogoway, T. (2019). *Kim Jong Un's Praetorian Guards Are Really A 100,000 Man Personal Army.* The War Zone. Retrieved April 2020 at https://www.thedrive.com/the-war-zone/21544/kim-jong-uns-pretorian-guards-are-really-a-100000-man-personal-army.
- Roozenburg, N.F.M. & Eekels, J. (1998). *Productontwerpen, structuur en methoden.* Utrecht: Lemma.
- Rosling, H., Rosling-Rönnlund, A. & Rosling, O. (2019) *Factfullness: Ten reasons we're wrong about the world – and why things are better than you think.* New York: Flatiron Books.
- Sanders, E.B.-N. & P.J. Stappers. (2012). *Convivial Toolbox: Generative Research for the Front End of Design.* Amsterdam: BIS Publishers.
- Sardar, Z. (2012). *De Nederlandse Fiets/ The Dutch Bike.* Rotterdam: nai010 Publishers.
- Sarkar, A. & Biswajit, P. (2016). The global menace of arsenic and its conventional remediation – a critical review. *Chemosphere,*158, 37–49.
- Schwartz, S.H. (2006, p.0). *Basic Human Values: An Overview.* Jerusalem: The Hebrew University of Jerusalem. Retrieved December 2014, from http://scholarworks.gvsu.edu/cgi/viewcontent.cgi?article=1116&context=orpc
- Schwarz, D. (1989). Visual Ethnography: Using photography in qualitative research. In *Qualitative Sociology,* 12(2) Summer, p.120.
- Siriaraya, P. Visch, V., Vermeeren, A. & Bas, M. (2018). A cookbook method for Persuasive Game Design. *International Journal of Serious Games,* 5(1), 37-71.
- Sleeswijk Visser, F. (2009). *Bringing the everyday life of people into design.* Doctoral thesis, Delft University of Technology, Delft.
- Snelders, D., Morel, K.P.N. & Havermans, P. (2011). The cultural adaptation of web design to local industry styles: A comparative study. *Design Studies,* 325, 457-481.
- Stinson T. (2018). *Cultural framing: Why context is crucial.* Retrieved at April 2020 from https://marumatchbox.com/cultural-framing-why-context-is-crucial/.
- Suri, J. and IDEO (2005). *Thoughtless acts.* Chronicle Books.
- Trompenaars F. & Hampden-Turner, C. (1998). *Riding the waves of culture; understanding diversity on global business.* New York: McGraw-Hill.
- Tuckman, B.W. (1965). Developmental sequence in small groups. *Psychological Bulletin, 63*(6), 384-399.
- Useem, R.H. & Downie, R.D. (1976). Third-Culture Kids. *Today's Education,* 65(3), 103-5.
- Uyttenbroek, E. & Versluis, A. (2002). *Exactitudes.* Rotterdam: 010 Publishers.
- van Boeijen, A.G.C. (2013). *Socio-cultural dimensions to sharpen designer's cultural eyeglasses.* In proceedings Engineering and Product Design Education conference, 5-6 September 2013, Dublin, Ireland.
- van Boeijen, A.G.C. (2014). *Cultural study in design: in search of a meaningful approach.* In proceedings Engineering and Product Design Education Conference, 4-5 September 2014, Enschede, The Netherlands.
- van Boeijen, A.G.C. (2015). *Card set: Crossing Cultural Chasms: Towards a culture-conscious approach to design.* Delft University of Technology, Delft. www.designandculture.info
- van Boeijen, A.G.C. (2015). *Crossing Cultural Chasms: Towards a culture-conscious approach to design.* Doctoral Thesis, Delft University of Technology, Delft.
- van Boeijen, A.G.C., Daalhuizen, J.J. & Zijlstra, J.J.M. (Eds.), (2020, Rev. ed.). *Delft Design Guide: Perspectives-Models-Approaches-Methods.* Amsterdam: BISPublishers.
- van Boeijen, A.G.C., Daalhuizen, J.J., Zijlstra, J.J.M. & van der Schoor, R. (Eds.), (2013). *Delft Design Guide.* Amsterdam: BISPublishers.
- Wann, D. L., Royalty, J., & Roberts, A. (2000). The Self-Presentation of Sport Fans: Investigating the Importance of Team Identification and Self-Esteem. *Journal of Sport Behavior,* 23(2).
- Wilkinson, C.R. & De Angeli, A. (2014). Applying user centred and participatory design approaches to commercial product development. *Design Studies,* 35 (6), 614–631.

Fenestrated axe blade, ca. early 2nd millennium BC.

BIS PUBLISHERS

Building Het Sieraad - Postjesweg 1 - 1057 DT Amsterdam - The Netherlands
T + 31 (0)20 515 02 30 - bis@bispublishers.com - www.bispublishers.com

AUTHOR: Annemiek van Boeijen
CO-AUTHOR, IMAGE RESERACH AND EDITING, GRAPHIC DESIGN: Yvo Zijlstra / Antenna-Men
REFERENCE: van Boeijen, A.G.C. and Zijlstra, I.S.J. (2020). *Culture Sensitive Design: A Guide to Culture in Practice.* Amsterdam: BIS Publishers.

ACKNOWLEDGMENTS

Adinda de Lange, thank you for your invaluable support. For one semester you were my assistant in setting up the structure and content of the book, in doing desk-top research, and in visualising a first draft for further discussion with the publisher and the graphic designer. Adinda is a designer at Zeewaardig Service Design.

Donna Devine, I had already thanked you in 2015 for your meticulous editing of my doctoral thesis. Thank you now for your dedicated assistance during the initial stages of the current book's development. Donna is a freelance English language copyeditor.

Kaila Vreeken, thank you for reading the very first draft. Your love of cultural diversity in combination with your pragmatic, designer-focused lens helped us to keep our attention fixed steadily on the target group. Kaila is a design researcher and service designer at MUZUS.

Design students, clients, and colleagues, thank you for sharing your real-world experiences. Every year, new students embark on bold and challenging projects that are increasingly internationally oriented and socially engaged. Clients and other initiators of design projects are of considerable value, sharing and learning together in this rich and compelling field of design.

ISBN 978 90 6369 561 3

The opening spread of the book shows a satellite image of agriculture in the Sahara desert, approximately 290 kilometres from the nearest city. Modern pivot irrigation technology with pump systems connected to sandstone water reserves, buried beneath the sand, make it possible to grow potatoes (darker green circles), wheat (lighter brown circles), and medicinal and aromatic plants, such as chamomile, in areas without rainfall. About 11,500 years ago, the art of cultivating plants and livestock marked the start and rise of sedentary human civilisations and cultures.

Image credits: Wikipedia; Wikimedia; Creative Commons; Nasa (p2-3); Roy Villevoye (p4, p69); Ryoji Iwata, Unsplash (p12); The Monkey Painter by Gabriel-Alexandre Decamps, 1833 (p16); Barbeque, Plainpicture/Linkimage (p16); Native American Haida shamans, photographed by Edward Dossetter in 1881, courtesy of the Royal BC Museum (p18); Pxhere (p26); Courtesy Nike (p27); Jacqueline Hassink (p37); Diego Delso (p40); Courtesy Beats by Dre (p45); Courtesy Mercedes Benz (p48); Yuchan Cal (p51); Mateo Garonne (p52); Allen Warren (p59); Lucy McRae (p61); Stocksy (p62); Juzo Itami (p72); Muerte del Maestro (Death of the Master) José Villegas Cordero, 1884 (p84); Aljandro Aravena / Elemental (p88); Stickansol (p99); Adobe Stock (p108); Max Stolznow (p112); Below the Surface, City council of Amsterdam, pfotography by Harold Strak (p114); Still from the role-playing game 'Final Fantasy' (p118); Marine Corps Sgt. Pete Thibodeau, US Department of Defense (p124); Publicityshot for Telenova *Santa Diabla* by Telemundo Studios, Miami (p139); The Infinite Recognition by René Magritte, 1963 (p126); Painting Vincenzo Camuccini, 1806 (p148); Ferdinant Porsche and Adolf Hitler, Alamy (p149); La Dolce Vita in Mali, photo by y Malick Sidibe (p150); Detail painting by Jacob van Ruijsdael (p152); Shutterstock (p155); Metropolitan Museum of Art (p158).

Captions: Source Wkipedia. Additional sources: Menand, 2019 (p16), Evancie, 2013 (p28), Wann et al., 2000 (p33), Hart, 2019 (p35), Basu, 2019) (p70), Popham, 2013 (p77), 'Talking to Strangers', Malcom Gladwell (p97), Campbell, 2019 (p120), Bezhan, 2012 (p124) - **Quotations:** Source Wkipedia. Additional sources: 1. Clifford Geertz; 2. Meiling, 2017; 3. Ro, 2019; 4. Baird & Hartter, 2017; 5. Klein & Sawchuk, 2000; 6. Puccio, Murdock and Mance, 2005; 7. Harris, 2016; 8. Hao Huang, 2011; 9. de Jongh, 2019; 10. Oatman-Stanford, 2012; 11. Jonathan Shockley; 12. The Guardian.